Elite • 68

The Military Sniper
since 1914

Martin Pegler · Illustrated by Ramiro Bujeiro

Consultant editor Martin Windrow

First published in 2001 by Osprey Publishing,
Midland House, West Way, Botley, Oxford OX2 0PH, UK
443 Park Avenue South, New York, NY 10016, USA
Email: info@ospreypublishing.com

CIP Data for this publication is available from the British Library

ISBN-13: 978-1-84176-141-1

Editor: Martin Windrow
Design: Alan Hamp
Originated by Valhaven, Isleworth, UK
Printed in China through World Print Ltd.
Typeset in Helvetica Neue and ITC New Baskerville

08 09 10 11 12 18 17 16 15 14 13 12 11 10

FOR A CATALOGUE OF ALL BOOKS PUBLISHED BY
OSPREY MILITARY AND AVIATION PLEASE CONTACT:

NORTH AMERICA
Osprey Direct, C/o Random House Distribution Center,
400 Hahn Road, Westminster, MD 21157, USA
E-mail: info@ospreydirect.com

ALL OTHER REGIONS
Osprey Direct UK, P.O. Box 140,
Wellingborough, Northants, NN8 2FA, UK
E-mail: info@ospreydirect.co.uk

www.ospreypublishing.com

Dedication

To Martin and Rosie Lloyd, whose courage and determination
are an inspiration to all of us.

Acknowledgements

No book is ever solely the work of the author, so I would like to
thank the following people, whose assistance I greatly appreciate:
Terry Champion, Geoff Cornish, Simon Dunstan, Martin Hinchcliffe,
Jonathan Moore, Joseph Ruckman, Gary Williams, Martin Windrow
and George Yannaghas. Also Andrew Evans-Hendrick of Riflecraft,
Bill Welch at Accuracy International, and snipers past and present
who preferred, for their own reasons, to remain anonymous.
  I am also indebted to the following publishers for kindly allowing
me to quote from their works: Betty Weston, of Messrs Robert Hale,
for permission to quote from *The Little Men* by K.W.Cooper,
published 1992; and Michael Greaves, of Ballantine Books, a
division of Random House Inc, for permission to quote from
Dead Centre by Ed Kugler, published 1999.

Dieu n'est pas pour les gros bataillons,
  mais pour ceux qui tirent le mieux.
'God is not on the side of the big battalions,
  but of the best shots.'   – *Voltaire*

Artist's Note

Readers may care to note that the original paintings from which the
colour plates in this book were prepared are available for private
sale. All reproduction copyright whatsoever is retained by the
Publishers. All enquiries should be addressed to:

Ramiro Bujeiro, C.C. 28, 1602 Florida, Argentina

The Publishers regret that they can enter into no correspondence
upon this matter.

THE MILITARY SNIPER SINCE 1914

INTRODUCTION

The snipe is a small, fast-flying game bird found in the marshes of Scotland and England, where it spends its winters. Renowned for its agile, twisting flight, it is an extraordinarily difficult target to shoot. A sportsman with a flintlock fowling gun who was able to bring down a snipe was considered to be an accomplished shot; and at some time during the mid-18th century the term 'snipe shooting' was simplified to 'sniping'. Nobody knows who first coined the phrase, or exactly when it came into common use; but by the late 19th century it was a well-established word for an above average sporting shot.

Today, 'sniper' is used indiscriminately by the media to refer to almost anyone who uses a rifle. This casual inaccuracy does the trained sniper a huge disservice; only a very few men and women have the unique blend of skills that will qualify them as snipers. To a great extent the technology they use is immaterial; a weapon with an optical sight attached does not instantly create a sniper, and many of the most effective snipers were just as competent with open 'iron' sights as they were with telescopic ones.

The term 'sniper' has always aroused mixed emotions, and many regard the whole concept of sniping with revulsion. Certainly, the sniper has been regarded with a deference bordering on unease even among combat soldiers. As Frederick Sleath, a sniping officer during World War I, commented, the infantrymen did not mix easily with his snipers '... for there was something about them that set them apart from ordinary men and made the soldiers uncomfortable.' – an attitude which prevails to the present day. Why this should be so is not easy to determine. Perhaps because many of us no longer admit to our primeval hunting instinct, the idea of stalking a human quarry is alien to us. We are, after all, educated into believing that all human life is sacrosanct, and the deliberate taking of life in peacetime is severely punished. For this reason comparatively few military snipers have talked or written about their experiences. When wars finish there is a natural tendency for attitudes towards killing to polarise; it does not take long before men who have served their country well are dismissed by the

A reconstructed militiaman of the American Revolutionary War. He wears a practical costume comprising a loose-fitting 'hunting shirt' with tight leggings and moccasins. His rifle is typical of the elegant long-barrelled, small calibre Pennsylvania rifles carried by Colonial sharpshooters. He carries a powder horn and pigskin bullet bag and has a hatchet thrust through his belt. (Courtesy Christine L. Malson-Ruckman)

A contemporary print of a British Volunteer rifleman of c1812, distinctive in his green uniform and black accoutrements, loading a Baker rifle. The powder flask seems, unusually, to be pushed into a breast pocket – not a feature of the uniform of the Regular army's 5/60th or 95th Rifles. Note, left background, the shako being employed as a shooting rest. (Courtesy National Army Museum, neg.28137)

ungrateful civilians they protected as little better than cold-blooded assassins. Whatever the reasons, the military sniper has rarely been lauded publicly as a hero, being regarded at best as an unpleasant necessity.

Such a response was, of course totally irrational when it was deemed perfectly acceptable in war to kill an enemy with high explosive shells, or randomly wipe out whole civilian communities with bombs. One reason for this discomfort was perhaps that among combat troops the sniper was unique in having the ability to hold life or death in the crosshairs of his sights. Few other soldiers ever had the questionable luxury of deciding who to kill, or when. Sergeant John Fulcher, a sniper in the US 36th Infantry Division in 1944, deliberated on his target as he watched a platoon of fresh German troops being marched up to the line. He made a logical decision:

'I cross haired the officer and shot him through the belly. He looked momentarily surprised. He plopped down on his butt in the middle of the road. He was dead by the time I brought my rifle down out of the recoil and picked him up again in my scope. His legs were drumming the road, but he was dead. His body just didn't know it yet.'

To the average soldier, war was a matter of obeying orders. Artillerymen pulled a lanyard, and somebody anonymous might die on the other side of the horizon; even the machine gunner usually fired at targets distant enough to allow a certain detachment; neither had any real idea of where their shells or bullets would land, or what damage they would do. They were largely able to treat the fighting as impersonal and to distance themselves from it. Combat sniping was not remote, as Vietnam sniping instructor Capt Robert Russell pointed out: 'Sniping is a very personal war, for a sniper must kill calmly and deliberately, shooting carefully selected targets, and must not be susceptible to emotions … they will see the look on the faces of people that they kill.'

Even the line infantryman fought on a different level, rarely having any personal animosity towards his enemy. He would do whatever he was ordered and in combat he reacted to circumstances, doing whatever it took to stay alive, to protect himself and his immediate comrades and, hopefully, to return home in one piece. He could certainly be killed, but even if he became a casualty statistically he was more likely to be wounded or captured, and his chances of survival were reasonable. A sniper's chances of survival were more capricious, for though many were wounded or killed as a result of enemy action few ever survived capture. Those who surrendered were invariably shot on the spot by their captors, whose fury had been stoked by their inability to retaliate as their comrades were picked off. Snipers understood the risks they took and were as keen to survive as anyone on the battlefield, putting considerable effort into planning their camouflage, positioning, and tactics.

Although a few snipers – particularly the Japanese – preferred to work on their own, the majority were not the lone wolves that they are often portrayed to be. The physical strain of being alone and close to an enemy for hours on end was normally too great for one individual, and it was quickly realised that the most successful snipers were those who worked in pairs, one to observe, the other to shoot. This was to become the *modus operandi* for most military sniping, although circumstances meant that this was never a hard and fast rule. Sniping is an art, not a science, and a true sniper requires an extraordinary range of skills. He must not only be an expert shot, but also excel at fieldcraft, observation and camouflage. More often than not the sniper will spend much of his time quietly observing and recording enemy activity before slipping away without firing a shot, having gained vital intelligence about troop movements, positions and the nature and size of enemy forces. He has to be a consumate professional, skilled, self-reliant and utterly confident. How did these skills come about, and why did sniping eventually become so pre-eminent on the 20th-century battlefield? To find an answer, we need to look back over three centuries at the technological changes that enabled the modern sniper to evolve.

THE FIRST SNIPERS

From medieval times until the middle of the 19th century most firearms were smoothbores, which in the case of the musket meant that it had an effective *aimed* range of no more than 80 yards. The loose-fitting ball was designed not for accuracy but for speed of loading and firing, and the effectiveness of the musket lay in its massed use as a close range volley fire weapon. Although the concept of the rifle had been well known since the 16th century, rifled barrels were very difficult and costly to manufacture. However, some 'marksmen' were present on the battlefields of Europe as early as the 17th century.

There are several accounts of men armed with sporting rifles being used during the English Civil War (1642-1648) to pick off officers, and the death of the charismatic Parliamentarian commander Lord Brooke during the siege of Lichfield in March 1643 is one of the better documented accounts from that war. Watching from their vantage point on the cathedral roof were two Royalist soldiers, one of whom, John Dyott, was armed with a very long-barrelled flintlock fowling gun. Lord Brooke, who was watching the firing of a cannon from the shelter of a house porch, leaned forward to observe the fall of shot. Dyott took careful aim and fired. The ball struck Brooke in the left eye, killing him

There were many variations on the long range 'back' position for firing the British Army's Baker rifle. In this reconstruction Private Eyles of the 95th Rifles uses his sling to brace his rifle while supporting his upper body on his pack. The legendary Tom Plunkett used a similar position to shoot General Colbert in 1809.

instantly. The distance, of about 150 yards, was not great; but Dyott was shooting a large calibre smoothbore musket, firing a home-made bullet cast from lead torn from the cathedral roof. By the standards of his day it was an extraordinarily fine shot.

Of course, at this date rare individuals such as Dyott did not in any sense comprise an organised sniping force. Most were countrymen, gamekeepers whose prowess with their muskets was learned during long years in the woods and fields of their home counties. Nevertheless they were a useful addition to the relatively unprofessional armies of their day, harassing the enemy by occasionally picking off the unwary. However, their numbers were tiny and their exploits had no overall effect on the general conduct of wars.

This was to change gradually after the Industrial Revolution, which gave gunsmiths access to mechanically powered machinery. New and more efficient barrel boring machines meant that rifled barrels could be made faster and cheaper. The problem was that the military authorities of the 18th century could conceive of no possible use for the rifle on the battlefield. All that was to change with the outbreak of hostilities between Britain and America in 1775. The British, ever mindful of their military tradition, expected to fight the colonists in the usual manner, in point blank confrontation. They did not expect the Americans to field riflemen clad in drab colours to act as scouts and skirmishers, picking off officers without ever exposing themselves to return fire. Frustratingly, the British suffered casualties without ever seeing who fired the shot or even where it came from. Not that it mattered: for the infantrymen to see their enemy was pointless, since the limited accurate range of their muskets left them incapable of returning fire.

The Americans were armed with Kentucky or Pennsylvania rifles – slender, long-barrelled, small calibre flintlocks with which they were as familiar as their own clothes. Most had learned to shoot accurately as children, bringing down small game and birds to help feed their families; and aimed shots at ranges of 300 yards were well within their capabilities. The British Land Pattern musket, with its inability to project a ball more than 200 yards, or accurately much more than a third of that distance, was useless when pitted against these rifles. Major George Hanger was the target of one American sharpshooter while conversing with the notorious Col Banastre Tarleton:

'A rifleman passed over the mill dam, evidently observing two officers and laid himself down on his belly; for in such positions

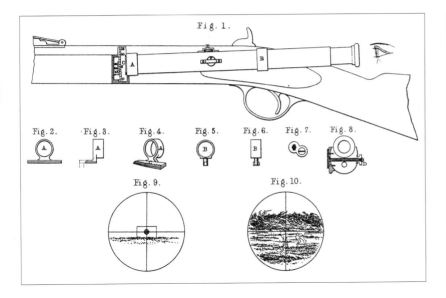

they always lie, to take a good shot at long distance. He took a deliberate and cool shot at my friend, at me and at our bugle-horn man ... Colonel Tarleton's horse and mine ... were not anything like two feet apart ... a rifle bullet passed between him and me; looking directly at the mill I observed the flash of powder ... the bugle-man jumped off his horse and said, 'Sir, my horse is shot.' I have passed several times over this ground and ... I can positively assert that the distance he fired at was full 400 yards.'

It is indicative of the attitude of contemporary soldiers towards musket fire that it did not occur to these officers to move, even when they realised that they were potential targets. Certainly, the feeling prevailed among many army officers that the practice of marksmen targeting individual officers was unfair and generally contrary to the rules of honourable warfare. On one occasion George Washington appeared within range of a British rifleman, who was instructed not to shoot, as it was not the business of common soldiers to target their social betters. It is interesting to speculate what might have happened to the course of world history if he had fired.

If the British regarded the American way of fighting as unfair, it could not be denied that in the heavily wooded country which comprised the eastern states it was very effective. A young British officer in the 70th Regiment of Foot by the name of Patrick Ferguson did finally convince the authorities that there was military value in the rifle, although he had to do it at his own expense. Grudgingly, the British government agreed that Ferguson could raise and train a rifle unit of 100 men, who adopted practical green uniforms and the skirmishing tactics of the Americans. Unfortunately their impact on the war was minimal, for in the wake of Ferguson's death during the battle of King's Mountain they and their rifles quietly faded from sight. Although Lord Howe went so far as to complain in Parliament about 'the terrible guns of the rebels', in reality the use of the rifle had little impact on the outcome of the war, which was decided by the conventional manoeuvres of a French expeditionary force with naval support. Its usefulness was soon forgotten, until a new threat appeared in Europe in the shape of Napoleon Bonaparte.

Pattern 1853 Enfield rifle in .577 calibre, with a brass-bodied Davidson Patent Telescopic Sight fitted to the left side. Its low, offset position did not make it particularly easy to use. Davidson had been fitting telescopic sights to hunting rifles since 1852. (Courtesy the Trustees of The Royal Armouries, object no.XII.2120)

7

THE AGE OF THE SHARPSHOOTER

By the end of the 18th century it was becoming obvious that the days of the musket as the exclusive weapon of the footsoldier were numbered, and the Board of Ordnance began to look rather more closely at the arms of the British soldier. In 1798 they ordered 5,000 Prussian-made rifle-muskets, of the Jäger type. The Jägers were an elite corps of riflemen serving in the German states, highly valued for their outstanding shooting and fieldcraft skills. Their heavy, short-barrelled rifles owed much to the design of the target guns that were popular in Prussia and Austria, but the quality of those supplied to Britain was poor, although some did find their way into the hands of the 60th Regiment and other foreign mercenary units. Although in agreement that some form of rifle should be adopted, the Board could not decide on the type of weapon required or indeed how it should be used. After lengthy trials at Woolwich in 1799 a design submitted by Ezekiel Baker was accepted. The first batch of 800 rifles were produced under contract in 1802, and issued to the newly formed 95th (Rifle) Regiment. These rifles were of similar style to the Jägers, manufactured in both 'musket bore' of .70in and 'carbine bore' of .62in; they were eventually adopted in the smaller calibre.

The riflemen who used them were not, in the accepted sense of the word, 'snipers', but worked as skirmishers – a concept which was at first alien to most regular Army officers, who believed that massed manoeuvres performed unquestioningly in obedience to orders were all that was required of an infantry soldier. The idea of a private soldier actually using his own initiative was a radical one, yet that was exactly what was required of the Riflemen. They were expected to use their skills to harass the enemy, taking up positions forward of their own front lines. A rifleman was trained to use the natural cover of the landscape, shoot his ammunition effectively and sparingly, and never give ground unless he could renew his offensive from another position. They fought in pairs or fours, spotting targets, confusing and demoralising the enemy, then melting into the background. From the point of view of the advancing enemy infantry, Riflemen were the devil incarnate. Most of the time they could not be seen, and even if they were they made poor targets for the smoothbore muskets of the infantry, who were forced to endure the stress of seeing comrades shot down around them without being able to retaliate. One anonymous Bonapartist officer's description of them is heavily reminiscent of the experience of later generations of soldiers in the two World Wars: 'I was sent out to skirmish against some of those in green –

Union sharpshooter Truman Head, alias 'California Joe', with his privately purchased M1859 breech-loading Sharps rifle. Fitted at the factory with special set triggers, this was the pattern eventually adopted for all of Berdan's Sharpshooters. Well past middle age, Head was honourably discharged from the US Army in November 1862 as a result of failing health. He should not be confused with another 'California Joe', Moses Milner, who served with Custer during the Indian Wars. (Courtesy Vermont Historical Society)

grasshoppers, I call them – you call them Rifle Men. They were behind every bush and stone, and soon made sad havoc amongst my men, killing all the officers in my company, and wounding myself, without [our] being able to do them any injury ...'

Although happy to set their riflemen to silencing artillery batteries by picking off their crews and horses well beyond musket range, many commanders still frowned upon the practice of deliberately targeting officers. Acceptance would grow in view of the effectiveness of such tactics. Although the accuracy of the Baker has been somewhat exaggerated over the years, there are a few well-documented accounts of accurate shooting at ranges of up to 300 yards, the most famous being that of Rifleman Thomas Plunkett of the 95th, who shot General Colbert at Villafranca during the retreat to Corunna on 5 January 1809. To manage such a feat Plunkett used the uncomfortable but effective 'back position'. Such shots required exceptional skill and the right conditions, and were not commonplace happenings.

In the context of early 19th-century warfare the rifle was certainly a precision weapon, but it had yet to come of age and there were still many lessons to be learned in its use. The Napoleonic Wars witnessed the introduction of the first properly trained military sharpshooting units, but their numbers were small and their training was in skirmishing, not sniping. Nevertheless, the tactics that they adopted – of observing the enemy's movements, and creating delays, harassment and confusion – were undoubtedly effective. Without knowing it they were forming the basis for the future deployment of the scout/snipers who were to become the specialists of the 20th-century battlefield. They had also been given the very practical distinction of wearing primitive 'camouflage' – green jackets rather than the traditional red, which stood out from the landscape like flaming beacons.

The Crimea and the American Civil War

As long as military doctrine, evolved during an age of inaccurate smoothbores, held that battles be fought face to face by large immobile bodies of men, then it was probably true that the cost of supplying the new rifles to soldiers outweighed the benefits. However, this dogmatic approach to tactics was to change forever with the introduction of the percussion lock rifled musket in the early 1830s, allied to a new form of industry called mass production. America led the way with highly mechanised arms manufacturing plants such as Springfield, Harper's Ferry and Colts at Hartford. Using these new manufacturing techniques meant that the production of comparatively cheap rifled military longarms was finally achievable. As a result, between about 1830 and

A group of British Rifle Volunteers, about 1870 – part of a national movement which swept the country. Individuals who went on to serve with the Regular Army from this background as experienced target shooters proved to be very able sharpshooters in the colonial wars of the late 19th century. All these are equipped with the .577 Snider, the first breech-loading centrefire rifle adopted by the British Army. (Courtesy National Army Museum, neg.4471/4)

1850 almost all the major military powers re-equipped their armies with percussion rifled muskets. Although still muzzle-loaded in the manner of all firearms dating back to the Middle Ages, the rifled barrels gave a potential level of accuracy up to ten times that of the smoothbore musket. At the same time the enclosed percussion lock, doing away with the business of priming with loose powder in all weathers, greatly improved reliability.

Britain adopted the Enfield-made Pattern 1851 Minié, subsequently to become the better known Pattern 1853. Initially in short supply, Minié rifles were issued only to the six best shots in each company; but they proved their worth. During the Cape Border Wars (1853) in South Africa, Private Wickens, a sharp-shooter, recalled that 'When the enemy began to show themselves … we opened fire … we made them move at a distance of 1,200 yards.' This is an extraordinary comment, considering that only 20 years before a soldier was regarded as safe from musket fire beyond 200 yards. The Crimean War (1853-1855) was to witness the birth of a new kind of warfare: trenches, sustained artillery bombardments, and infantry firing at each other with accurate rifles at ranges previously only attainable by artillery. The problem was not range but simply identifying the target at such extreme distances, bearing in mind that a standing man at 1,000 yards is considerably smaller than the area covered by the foresight of a rifle. While serving in the Crimea LtCol D.Davidson, a keen rifle shooter of the 1st City of Edinburgh Rifle Volunteers, observed with interest the combined efforts of two riflemen in the trenches at Sebastopol who had unwittingly formed the perfect sniping partnership: 'One soldier was observed lying with his rifle carefully pointed at a distant embrasure and with his finger on the trigger ready to pull, while by his side lay another with a telescope directed at the same object. He, with the telescope, was anxiously watching the moment when a [Russian] gunner should show himself, in order that he might give the signal to fire.' Partly as a result of this experience, Davidson patented an early telescopic sight, which could be fitted to any rifle.

Despite technical advances, muzzle-loading rifles still suffered from a number of inherent faults. The black powder absorbed moisture like a sponge, fouled the barrels badly and left a telltale cloud of white smoke when fired, as obvious to an enemy as waving a flag. They were also slow to reload, forcing a man to either stand up or roll to one side and perform prone gymnastics to ram home the powder and ball.

Of particular interest is the primitive – and unnamed – optical sight fitted to the Marshall Tidd rifle illustrated on page 9, of about 1.5x power with a very narrow field of view. The pillar screw adjustment for elevation and windage, although not particularly robust, is both simple and efficient. (Courtesy Roy Jinks)

If the tactical potential of accurate long-range shooting was not entirely appreciated by the senior army commanders of the day, it was soon being argued by energetic enthusiasts in a number of countries, and notably in America. The outbreak of hostilities between the Union North and Confederate South in 1861 signalled the start of the biggest conflict ever witnessed in America, and one in which the rifle was to become the most important and potent military arm ever used. At the start of the war the manufacturing technology was already in place to provide excellent quality, accurate rifles to both sides, entirely suitable for sniping. The problem was persuading the field commanders that there was a need. The North had the advantage of having both the money and availability of weapons, most manufacturing companies being under Union control; thus the US Army was the first to raise and equip a specialist regiment, when in June 1861 the 1st Regiment of Sharpshooters was formed under the command of Col Hiram Berdan.

'Berdan's Sharpshooters' were trained specifically for sniping and scouting, and so many clamoured to join that eventually two regiments were formed. The men who joined Berdan were all expert shots who had to pass a rigid shooting test: 'No man is admitted who does not shoot, at 600 feet distance, ten consecutive shots at an average of five inches from the bull's eye. Not a man is accepted, under any circumstances, who varies a hair-breadth from the mark.' Remarkable though it may seem, many men exceeded this proficiency. After much lobbying by Col Berdan the Ordnance Department equipped the unit with the breech-loading Sharps rifle in 1862. The Sharps had an enviable reputation for reliability and accuracy but, contrary to popular belief, only a few of the 1,500 rifles supplied to the Sharpshooters were ever equipped with any form of optical sight (and neither did the regiment's name originate from their use of the Sharps). Berdan's men were equipped with the same basic uniform and equipment as all line infantry of the period, although in green rather than Union blue. In an attempt to make the most of their skills they were employed as specialist troops attached to brigades, to be used wherever was most necessary.

The Confederate Army was equally well endowed with skilled shots, the majority of its men coming from rural backgrounds where the ability to hit a running squirrel with a snap shot, or kill a deer after careful stalking, were considered to be normal skills. However, the organisation of the Confederate forces was not as rigid as that of the Union; and while Berdan's regiments were a distinct part of the North's army the sharp-shooters in the Confederate militia and independent units mainly served within the mass of line infantry. As the war progressed, however, some formally recruited sharpshooting units were raised, such as the 1st Company South Carolina Volunteers, the 30th Virginia Battalion, and the Palmetto Sharpshooters. The most outstanding battalion shots could be given the chance to compete against their fellows for the highly valued prize of an English Enfield or Whitworth rifled musket. Of all of the weapons used the Whitworth was arguably the most accurate and desirable. The problem was that they were also extraordinarily expensive, partly because of the difficulty of smuggling them through the Union's naval blockade. A basic Whitworth cost $600 and a cased example with an optical sight almost $1,000, compared to $150 for a P53 Enfield and $42 for a Sharps. Although the Whitworth has achieved almost mythical status, the numbers used by the South were very small, probably no more than 175 – a tiny proportion compared to the number of Enfields or Sharps in Confederate hands.

There are many accounts of the efficiency of sharpshooters during the Civil War, but one of the best documented was the death of Union Gen John Sedgewick during the battle of Spotsylvania on 19 May 1864. Overseeing the placement of artillery behind the lines, he saw his men becoming unnerved by near misses from sharpshooters. Pointing at the distant rebel lines he called out, 'They couldn't hit an elephant at this distance!' – at which point he fell from his horse, having been struck by a bullet below the left eye. An account by a soldier of the South Carolina sharpshooters mentions the event from the Confederate side: 'This very same day Ben Powell came in and told us that he had killed, or wounded a high ranking Yankee officer. He said that he had fired at a very long range at a group of horsemen whom he recognised as officers. At his shot one fell from his horse, and the others dismounted and bore him away. That night the enemy's pickets called over to ours that General John Sedgewick, commanding the 6th Corps was killed that day by a Confederate sharpshooter.' It was an impressive shot, particularly because Sedgewick was mounted and moving and the rifle used was unlikely to have been fitted with a telescopic sight.

It was coincidental that it was around this time that optical science had begun to emerge from the Middle Ages, and better quality telescopic sights were being fitted to the new rifled muskets, providing a slightly magnified image of perhaps 1.5x power and enabling the shooter to identify and shoot at a target otherwise too distant for the naked eye. The scopes were unsophisticated; focusing was by means of an adjustable eyepiece in the manner of a telescope, magnification was low, the field of vision was very narrow, and while there was normally a means of adjusting elevation no form of windage adjustment was provided. There were a number of American optical sight manufacturers such as Alvin Clark of Boston and Morgan James of New York, but any rifle equipped with an optical sight was at that time a rare and expensive item.

What became of these sharpshooters and their rifles with the cessation of hostilities in 1865? The answer is one that was to be repeated over and over again during the following century, as the exigencies of war diminished and the sharpshooter's services were dispensed with. No attempts were made to pass on to the regular army the skills that had been learned by these specialists, and they returned to their homes, taking their knowledge and their rifles with them. But if military thinking stagnated for decades after the war, technology certainly did not.

For decades firearms manufacturers and inventors had chased two Holy Grails: to create a smokeless propellant, and to perfect the design of the breech-loading rifle. Curiously, the achievement of both was to virtually coincide, ushering in a new technological era that would enable the sniper to come of age. The invention of a smokeless propellant – Nitrated Cellulose – was perfected in France in 1886; not only did it burn more efficiently, creating higher pressures and greater velocities, but it was unaffected by moisture, and when fired gave off only a discreet puff of grey smoke. Breech-loading weapons had been around for a long time, and many different patterns had been used in the American Civil War. By the outbreak of the Franco-Prussian War in 1870 the concept had been perfected, and by 1900 most of the world's armed forces had adopted the breech-loading bolt action magazine rifle, chambering a relatively small calibre centrefire cartridge loaded with the new propellant. The list of manufacturers was almost endless: Mauser, Krag, Mannlicher, Enfield, Schmit-Rubin, Remington – all produced accurate, beautifully made military rifles capable of shooting out to ranges of 2,000 yards. The rifle had been refined to the point at which it was to survive virtually unchanged until just a generation ago; and rifles made for World War I are still in effective use today in some of the more unsophisticated corners of the world.

It was an untrained amateur army of Boer farmers who were to demonstrate what could be achieved with the new generation of rifles, proving that a small number of highly skilled marksmen without the need for any technology other than good weapons and sharp eyes could run rings around a large, well-trained professional army. The Boers had spent their lives on the open veldt, tracking and shooting game for food; and they found no difficulty in shooting British soldiers at such extreme ranges that their victims could not tell where the shots were coming from, let alone see their assailants. It is interesting to note that one of the most frequently reported problems by officers and men was their inability to see the Boer sharpshooters even when their location was known. Targets could not be identified because most Boers were bearded and wore shapeless dark slouch hats which effectively combined to obscure their faces. It was an early, though accidental, example of a camouflage that was to be copied in later years. By the end of the Boer war in 1901 the British Army had been taught a sharp lesson in the deficiencies of their long-range marksmanship. Although musketry training was vigorously pursued in the next decade, little of what had been learned specifically about sniping seems to have been remembered when World War I broke out.

Boer 'commandos' of the South African War, 1899-1901, with an interesting selection of rifles. These include, from the left, three 7mm Orange Free State Mauser M1885/6; front centre, 8mm Portuguese Guedes, based on the Martini action; second from right, .303in Lee Metford Mk I. Some of the Boers are very young indeed. (Courtesy National Army Museum, neg.85364)

German Scharfschützen Gewehr 98 in use. The sniper has the leather case for the telescopic sights on his belt. This is doubtless a posed photo, as neither man would normally expose his head so blatantly in a front line position by 1916 – the date of issue of the steel helmet. (Courtesy Bundesarchiv)

The Jäger tradition

As the fighting of the first months slowed to stalemate in late 1914, both sides dug in and a war of attrition began. The trenches became a haven for snipers; and the Germans excelled at this skill, dominating No Man's Land by the end of that year. So accomplished were they that the most innocuous things could result in unwelcome attention, as Lt S.Shingleton, of the British 7th Divisional Artillery recorded in his postwar reminiscences. He noted that on the night of 3 February 1915, ' … to be seen standing in the open meant instant death from a sniper's bullet. It was even dangerous to wear a luminous wrist watch, for the light from same could be seen a long way off in the pitch darkness; a few snipers' bullets had whistled past us, and the RE officer in charge suggested that my luminous watch was the cause whereupon I promptly put it in my pocket.' One British sniper officer reckoned that exposing any part of the body for more than three seconds would result in a shot from a German sniper, and they had no shortage of targets.

In 1914 the British Army arguably had the best trained rapid fire riflemen of any country in the world, each capable of delivering 15 aimed shots a minute in volley fire at battle ranges. This skill might have won the war in six months if open warfare had continued, but it did not. British musketry training had put little emphasis on developing individual marksmanship, leaving the BEF largely unable to retaliate in kind to the German sniper scourge. Worse, most soldiers failed to understand how deadly snipers were, despite strategically placed trench signs and dire warnings from veterans. Newly arrived recruits could not help but satisfy their curiosity by peeking over the parapet, inevitably collapsing limply with a bullet through the head. On any day in 1915 a single battalion in a quiet sector would lose an average of 12 to 18 men through sniping. So dominant were the Germans that in one region near the Aubers Ridge in 1915, a bored sniper amused himself over the course of several days by shooting a large cross pattern into the wall of a ruined cottage behind the British front line, without fear of retribution.

This haemorrhage of manpower, and the psychological impact on the troops of the constant losses, began to concern front line officers deeply. For the most part all that could be done to deal with a particularly troublesome sniper was to call down shelling on his suspected position – assuming the artillery had enough shells available for such minor tasks. There was hope, however; many officers, such as Maj F.M.Crum of the King's Royal Rifle Corps, had been on the receiving end of the Boers' shooting during the South African War and were only too well aware of the value of sniping. As Crum later wrote: 'My first visit to the trenches left a lasting impression on me ... wherever we had been in the front trenches, the tops of sandbags were being constantly ripped by bullets and periscopes being broken. Bullets were ringing on an iron loophole plate our men had inserted in the parapet ... The Colonel put his periscope up. It was shot at once and he got a knock in the face.'

A British early wartime training photograph, c1915, showing the difference that camouflage makes. The soldier on the left stands out clearly; there is a second man to the right of the picture who is almost invisible – the muzzle of his SMLE is just visible in the foliage below the 'lump' of his hooded head.

The problem for Britain was in finding and training enough snipers to turn the tables. In 1914 Germany was the only major combatant country with access to a good supply of telescopically sighted rifles and men to use them. In Germany, unlike Britain, hunting was a popular social pastime and the vast forests provided a very wide range of game. As a result the use of rifles fitted with telescopic sights was far more common than it was in Britain, where only a rare few big-game hunters or Highland deer-stalkers had access to and experience of such weapons. On the outbreak of war the German military were therefore able to quickly requisition several hundred suitable sporting rifles, as well as issuing upwards of 15,000 Mauser Gewehr 98 service rifles with factory-fitted scopes. There was a ready-trained cadre of potential snipers available from men whom had spent their lives in the forests as gamekeepers, or had followed a hunting tradition from boyhood. They understood the importance of using the terrain to its best advantage, the effective use of camouflage and, above all, the need for patience. Germany had long encouraged the best shots in every battalion to enter for sniper training at one of several schools. Battalion sniper sections usually comprised 24 men, who were free to pick their own positions anywhere they chose. As a result they roamed No Man's Land at will, inflicting heavy casualties on the British and French. When firing from the trenches they used bulletproof steel loophole plates set into the parapets, which proved a tricky problem for British snipers who had no access to armour-piercing ammunition. Initially they could only retaliate by using privately acquired, large bore, high velocity hunting rifles, mostly of over .350in calibre, capable of punching through the steel.

British sniper training

In a makeshift attempt to remedy the problem in February 1915 some 52 sporting rifles were purchased by the War Office from commercial suppliers for issue to British snipers. Although Britain lagged behind, things were to change due to the persistence of experienced officer-riflemen such as F.M.Crum, H.Hesketh-Pritchard, N.A.Armstrong and others. Hesketh-Pritchard, a prewar hunter and avid exponent of the art of sniping, realised very quickly that most of the telescope-equipped rifles then in service were being used by men who lacked the most basic

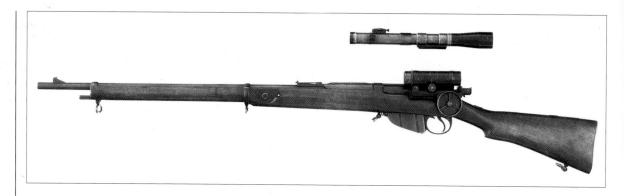

knowledge of even how to zero them. As most snipers had never had any formal instruction in the adjustment or care of telescopic sights, it was hardly surprising that six out of every ten sniping rifles issued in 1915 were reckoned to be unserviceable within a month. Worse, no training was given in camouflage or fieldcraft. Pritchard recounted how, in an early tour of the lines, he observed one British sniper with a scoped rifle bobbing up over the parapet to fire a snapshot at the German lines – a practice that would guarantee him a very brief service career.

Under pressure from like-minded officers, High Command began to appreciate that organising and training their own snipers would not only enable them to contest control of No Man's Land, but would also reduce casualties and dramatically raise morale. As a result of enthusiastic backing from the Corps Commander, the First Army SOS School (Sniping, Observation and Scouting) was set up at Bethune in 1915, to be shortly followed by the formation of the Second Army School of Sniping. The syllabus, which then lasted 17 days, was to set the standard for sniper training to the present day. Care and maintenance of rifles and scopes was followed by shooting assessment, using ordinary service rifles and open sights on a wide variety of target types, concentrating on both accuracy and speed of response. It was fully appreciated by the instructors that barrel life, and thus accuracy, were much reduced the more a rifle was fired. Pritchard typically felt that 500 rounds was the maximum that could be fired before accuracy suffered appreciably. A thorough familiarisation with the methods of zeroing a rifle was taught, as well as estimating distance and wind strength – these last being by far the most difficult skills to acquire, which sometimes deceived even experienced snipers. Observation and the use of the scout telescope was followed by map reading, patrolling and scouting, including the use of ground and cover, camouflage and the construction of sniper posts. Theoretical and practical work were followed by a stiff examination.

It was found that many good target shooters were totally unsuited to sniper training because their mentality was geared purely to static

A British sniper in France, 1915. He wears a knitted 'cap, comforter' rather than the service cap, and over his shoulder he carries leather binocular and telescopic sight cases. His rifle is an SMLE Mk III with Periscopic Prism scope offset to the left. (Courtesy Imperial War Museum, neg.HU72876)

An Australian sniping post at Gallipoli, 1915. Private Billy Sing, the famous AIF sniper, looks back at the camera, while his observer uses a scout telescope to spot for targets. Sing used a standard SMLE with 'iron' sights, proving that telescopic sights were not a prerequisite for a good sniper. (Courtesy Australian War Memorial, neg.C00429)

shooting, not stalking and killing. Unsurprisingly the most successful snipers turned out to be deer-stalkers, small game hunters and gamekeepers whose shooting, though good, was not necessarily to Bisley standards. Major N.A. Armstrong, who became commandant of the 2nd SOS, commented that the best men were 'game hunters, trappers, prospectors, surveyors, lumberjacks and poachers'. The best natural snipers were found amongst the Australians, Canadians and – ironically – South Africans. All came from countries where a rifle was considered an essential tool and where hunting for food or sport was an everyday act. However, over time the sniping schools turned out many excellent snipers who did not enjoy the advantage of such a background.

It was not only in France and Flanders that sniping was beginning to have a significant effect on morale. The landings at Gallipoli in June 1915 quickly turned into a microcosm of the stalemate in France. In trenches less than 100 yards apart, British, Australian and New Zealand troops faced a Turkish enemy who proved considerably tougher and more competent than anyone had expected. The Turks had many excellent snipers in their ranks and despite having no optically equipped rifles they made life very hard for the invaders. Author A.P.Herbert daily witnessed the result of their expertise: '… We lost 12 men each day; they fell … shot through the head, and lay snoring horribly in the dust; and in the night there were sudden screams where a sentry had moved his head too often against the moon.' Neither did the Allied forces have access to proper sniping rifles, so sniping was done with open sights – a task at which the Australian kangaroo-hunters excelled.

Some men had those special qualities that made them snipers rather than sharpshooters, and the Australians had more than their fair share. Probably the best documented was a Queenslander of Indian origin, Billy Sing. A small, unassuming man, he was considered unusual for always preferring to work with a partner, unknowingly following a trend that had started a century beforehand. Aside from being a natural shot, he was possessed of legendary patience, and would hold his fire until his observer considered that his victim had exposed sufficient of his body to make a certain kill; Sing would only shoot on hearing the command 'Right!' from his mate. His confirmed score at Gallipoli was well over 150.

British sniper tactics

In early 1915 the British began to organise their own battalion sniper sections consisting of 16 snipers, a sergeant and a corporal. Like their German counterparts, snipers were excused normal trench duties and could position themselves anywhere they thought useful. They might

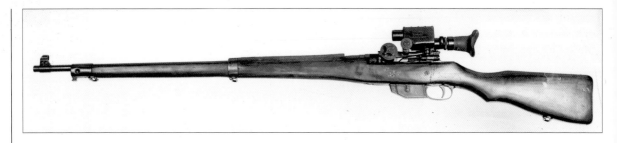

The .303in Canadian M1910 Ross rifle fitted with a Warner & Swasey sight. The Ross's straight-pull bolt did not work well in the trenches, but it proved to be a very good sniping rifle. A number of different telescopic sights were fitted, this being one of the rarer examples. (Courtesy Geoffrey Brown)

1915 patent drawing of the most common British telescopic sight of World War I, made by the Periscopic Prism Co. The scope and mount (E) were dovetailed, and slid into a female block (D), which was screwed and soldered to the receiver of the rifle. The scope could be instantly removed by depressing the spring catch (D5) – which made the War Office's insistence on offset scopes, supposedly so as not to prevent normal battlefield rapid reloading and fire, fairly inexplicable. (Patent Office)

crawl into camouflaged positions in No Man's Land, or divide the German line into sectors, spending the day watching for enemy movement and gathering information. Unlike the German snipers, who carried binoculars and often worked alone, the Sniping Schools taught that British snipers should always work in pairs, sniper and observer swapping roles periodically to avoid eyestrain. They were introduced to the very powerful 20x power telescope, which took considerable skill and training to master, but was unequalled for clarity and distance observation. Much of this vital training was given by the men of the Lovat Scouts, a unique unit of about 200 men raised primarily from Highland gamekeepers or 'ghillies'. Their powers of observation were legendary and they were capable, when visibility permitted, of spotting enemy troop movement with their telescopes at distances of up to ten miles. Their experience in deer-stalking meant that they could identify hidden targets invisible even to a trained sniper. As Hesketh-Pritchard once said of them, 'If they reported a thing, the thing was as they reported it.'

Camouflage became a vitally important element of sniping, and the Lovats were to introduce a new term – 'ghillie suit' – to the sniper's language. For years they had used this to enable them to stalk game. It comprised a loose hessian (burlap) robe covered in tufts of brown and green material and bundles of grass that blended into the landscape to the extent that an observer could not spot a man wearing one at ten feet. It was to become a favourite garment of British snipers through two World Wars, and has been adopted in one form or another by almost every other country. Camouflage netting was also popular, being light, cool and easy to obtain. Snipers also found other ingenious means of hiding. Hollow metal trees, dummy corpses, hollowed-out logs and specially constructed underground lairs all became their preserve. By the end of the Great War the tactical role of the sniper had broadened into that of scout/sniper. Troop movements, potential duped targets for artillery, the

A.D. 1915. Feb. 24. No. 3027.
PERISCOPIC PRISM CO. & another's COMPLETE SPECIFICATION.

locations of machine gun posts or command positions and the identification of enemy units were all vital information for HQ Staffs, whose eyes and ears the snipers had become.

Optical sights and service rifles

Accurate long-range shooting was always limited by the ability of the shooter to identify his target. Although the scout telescopes were efficient instruments, the same cannot be said of the optical sights initially available to the British. Before 1914 a number of simple clip-on 2x power sights such as the Commons, Lattey, Martin, Gibbs and Neill had been tested on the Army's recently adopted .303in Mk I Short Magazine Lee Enfields. They worked on the Galilean magnifying principle, but their tiny 1¼ degree field of view and vulnerability made them impractical, although they were better than nothing. The first really effective British military telescopic sight was a 2x power unit produced by the Periscopic Prism Company and approved on 4 May 1915. It was fitted to both the SMLE No.1 Mk III and Pattern 1914 No.3 Mk I (T) rifles, and as supplies of these rifles to the front increased the situation began to improve for the British snipers. As Maj Crum noted gleefully in 1915: 'With a telescopic sight … the most perfect sighting can be got upon an inconspicuous object, and without any waste of time. I have frequently seen a head over the parapet through glasses [binoculars] and then tried to locate it with an ordinary rifle, and found that it was too indistinct to be visible.' A great number of different scopes were fitted to the SMLE during the war, the most common being the Periscopic Prism, 3x power Aldis and 5x power Winchester, although a number of prominent sporting rifle manufacturers such as Rigby, Holland & Holland, Gibbs and Purdey also supplied and fitted scopes to service rifles.

Aside from Germany, the only other country to enter the war with a telescope-equipped rifle was the United States, which had a number of Springfield M1903 rifles fitted with a 5.2x power Warner & Swasey prismatic scope. The bulky Warner & Swasey had some unfortunate design faults, for with an eye relief of just 1.5 inches a rubber pad was required to protect the shooter's brow from 'scope bite', caused when the recoiling eyepiece of the scope strikes the eyebrow so hard as to cut it. It was said of the Warner & Swasey that 'it could make a flincher out of a cigar store Indian'. Its prism also magnified any dirt that entered, a small piece of grit appearing to be a house-brick when viewed through the eyepiece. It was also affected by moisture – although in fairness all telescopic sights, even the better quality German scopes, suffered to a greater or lesser degree in the damp conditions of trench warfare, fogging up

The parapet of a German trench seen from No Man's Land, complete with general detritus including two steel sniper's plates. These are simply dummies to attract the attention of Allied marksmen. The real sniper's position is the apparently half-empty sandbag in the lower left foreground, forming the lower point of a rough diamond shape with the lumps of concrete. This has an angled aperture leading back into the trench.

An interesting picture of four US Army scout-snipers wearing home-made 'ghillie suits'. Their Springfields do not have scopes mounted, but their M1907 leather shooting slings can be seen. These gave good arm bracing; adopted by Allied snipers through both World Wars, they are still in use today. (Courtesy US National Archives, Signal Corps Collection)

at infuriatingly inopportune moments (a problem that was still plaguing snipers 70 years later).

In technical terms, there was little to choose between the rifles used by the warring countries; none had adopted a sniping rifle based on an existing commercial design, although there were plenty of manufacturers who could have provided such weapons. The argument against using commercial rifles was naturally that of cost, so standard production service rifles were selected. The 7.92mm Mauser Gewehr 98 was generally believed to be the best, partly due to its selection process, whereby only rifles that had proved particularly accurate during testing were chosen. In addition its longer barrel and smoother bolt action made it arguably the most competent sniping weapon. Despite its subsequent fame, the British .303in SMLE was something of a compromise, being a relatively short-barrelled design for use by both infantry and mounted units. This proved a mixed blessing, for although it was lighter and easy to handle neither the all-enclosing woodwork nor the short barrel aided accuracy, and some found the bolt action awkward. The American M1903 Springfield was a well made bolt action rifle chambered for the .30-06in calibre cartridge. It was a good rifle, but as no selection process was applied to weapons taken from production lines some Springfields proved less satisfactory than others when modified for sniping. Accuracy could vary wildly and while in theory those that did not meet requirements were to be returned to general service, in practice this seldom happened since scope-equipped sniping rifles were in such short supply.

Finding a reliable telescopic sight was only a part of creating an accurate rifle. Just as important was the bedding of the barrel, to ensure it was rigid, the smoothness of the action and trigger and the means by which the scope was mounted to the rifle. Military rifle barrels were invariably surrounded by woodwork, which could swell when wet, causing a loss of accuracy. Triggers and actions were simply as they left the factory and some were better than others, the Mausers generally being regarded as the best. Scope mounts needed to be strong, for the slightest play would make it impossible to retain zero. German makers such as Zeiss, Gerard and Voigtlander had pioneered an efficient means of securing the scopes to rifles, using hooked feet known as claw mounts which locked into slotted, machined mounts fitted above the receiver of the rifle. These mounts were not only strong, but also placed the telescopic sight in the best position – above the receiver directly in line with the sniper's right eye.

In Britain the War Office, apparently mesmerised by the fear that snipers would single-handedly have to face massed ranks of enemy infantry, insisted that all telescopic sights be mounted offset to the left to permit charger-loading of the magazine and use of the open sights. This offset required the shooter to adopt an awkward canted posture. As snipers usually only fired one carefully aimed shot at a time and the scopes were quickly detachable anyway, the War Office requirement was bizarre, and resulted in a continual stream of complaints from front-line sniper units. One unforeseen side effect was that a standard steel loophole could not be used, as the sniper would have no sight picture through the aperture. Hesketh-Pritchard had practical experience of the disadvantage of this system: 'There was a sniper beside me who had one of my rifles, a Mauser which had a telescope sight on the top, and with which he was able to fire through his loophole … a working party of Germans appeared … they had but a few yards to go to retain their own trench. The sniper who was next to me got off a shot, but two of the snipers armed with the government weapons [i.e. with offset scopes] … who were waiting at loopholes, found that neither of them could bring their rifles to bear at the extreme angle at which the Germans were disappearing.'

Unlike the German rifles, the early war scope mounts fitted to British rifles were not factory-designed, being a wartime expedient created and

An extraordinary photograph which captures the split second in which a British gunner, still clutching the firing lanyard, topples backwards as he is shot by a sniper in Salonika. The dust from the impact of the bullet on his tunic is visible against the dark shadow of the gunshield at lower right. (Crown copyright)

manufactured by the different scope makers to fit the SMLE and P14, and generally they were not as strong as those of the Mausers. By 1918 these problems had largely been solved with the introduction of the No.3 Mk I* (T) rifle, a P14 Enfield equipped with an Aldis No.4 sight. This had solid mounts fitted to the receiver and rear sight platform in the manner of the Mauser rifles, and it proved a fine combination, many seeing active service again in World War II and beyond.

Ranges and ammunition

As is so often the case where a shooting skill is involved, many exaggerated claims have been made about the abilities of snipers during the Great War to hit targets at extreme ranges. Most trench sniping was done at ranges of less than 200 yards and snipers who occupied positions in No Man's Land could be considerably closer. Snipers working from behind the lines certainly shot at greater distances, anywhere from 300-500 yards; but bearing in mind the limited magnification of most scopes, this was pretty near to the limit for accurate, one-shot, one-hit shooting. A German instruction document printed in early 1915 reinforces this, stating that 'The weapons with telescopic sights are very accurate up to 300 metres'.

Hesketh-Pritchard also had something to say on the use of a scoped rifle in anything other than perfect conditions: 'The chances of hitting a German head at 600 yards ... if there is any wind blowing at all, are not great. We therefore ... never went back further than 400 yards, and our greatest difficulty was to teach the snipers to appreciate the strength of the wind.' Then, as now, it was a matter of experience tinged with a little guesswork to hit a small target at 200 yards in a strong wind, and skilled snipers preferred to work at dawn or dusk, when the light was sharper and there was little or no breeze. The light-gathering properties of the scopes meant that dawn and dusk were referred to as 'first and last scope light', when there was just sufficient light to pick out a target. Generally, it was felt that a head shot at 200 yards and a body shot at 400 were good levels of accuracy to achieve.

For the intended victim, being as far away from the sniper as possible was the best option, for none survived close range head shots. Siegfried Sassoon was fortunate in his encounter with a sniper in April 1917: '... I thought what a queer business it all was, and then decided to take a peep at the surrounding country. No sooner had I popped my head out of the sap than I received what seemed like a tremendous blow in the back – between the shoulders. My first notion was that I had been hit by a bomb from behind. What had really happened was

A World War II German Army sniper on the Eastern Front aims a short side-rail K98k, bracing its stock with his left hand. Snipers adopted whatever shooting position enabled them to achieve the steadiest aim; placing the fore-end of the rifle on a solid rest was always preferable to freehand shooting. Both men wear 'splinter' camouflage helmet covers, and the sniper a camouflaged winter jacket; the effect is rather negated by his NCO observer's fully badged tunic complete with Close Combat Clasp. (Courtesy Bundesarchiv)

Clad in winter camouflage, one of Russia's highest scoring World War II snipers, Vasily Zaitsev (left), gives instruction to a couple of trainee snipers or *zaichata* - 'leverets'. A shepherd from the Urals, Zaitsev was credited with 149 kills. His Moisin rifle has the 4x power PT sight fitted. (Courtesy Arkhiv Muzeya Panorami Stalingradskoy Bitvi)

that I had been sniped from in front. Anyhow my attitude towards life and the war had been instantly and completely altered for the worse.' The soldier/poet was very lucky indeed, for the bullet was quite likely aimed at his head, but passed through his chest without hitting any vital organs.

Counter-sniping had become a priority and sniper confrontations were invariably brief and fatal. Frederick Sleath, a sniping officer in the 51st Highland Division, recorded a duel between himself and a German sniper somewhere in the Ypres Salient in 1916. As he took aim from a loophole the German fired, the shot striking the steel plate two inches from Sleath's face. Recovering and taking aim again, his finger was just squeezing the trigger when a second shot from the German struck the steel loophole. The shock made Sleath involuntarily complete the trigger pull, cursing the wasted shot. He was startled by his sergeant's shout, '"You've hit him, sir. God, look at his rifle." He could see a large white splinter from the wooden casing of the rifle barrel lying below the loophole, and the rifle itself was cocked up in the air by the weight of the butt and slowly slithering out of sight into the trench.'

No special ammunition was issued to snipers, although the consistent accuracy of carefully prepared match-grade cartridges was well known to competition shooters. However, the Ministry of Munitions felt that the logistics involved in providing small quantities of such ammunition to snipers was impractical. Snipers always zeroed their rifles using one particular batch of ammunition, and they kept a very close eye on their own supplies. As long as that batch lasted, the rifle should not require zeroing again unless the scope was knocked. Although powerful – a .303in bullet would penetrate 18ins of clay-packed sandbag at 200 yards – ordinary ball ammunition could not defeat armoured plates; and in 1915 German snipers were issued limited quantities of S.m.K armour-piercing cartridges for use against steel loopholes and machine guns, giving them a considerable technical advantage. Allied snipers were not officially issued with AP ammunition, but from late 1916, as it became progressively easier to obtain, many snipers would carry a few rounds for use against 'hard' targets.

As the war progressed and their skill grew the effectiveness of the snipers increased commensurately. There are no statistics to show just how effective sniping actually was, or any record of the numbers of soldiers to whom a second's carelessness brought death from a sniper's bullet; they simply joined the lists of 'killed in action'. But some inkling of how efficient snipers could be can be gleaned from the fact that between New Year and March 1918 the snipers of the British 38th Division – i.e. nine battalion sections – made 387 confirmed kills. Incalculable, too, was the moral and psychological effect on men of knowing that there was a sniper in the vicinity. Within 20 years another conflict began that would see sniping not just as a response, but as an important tactical function of every major combatant power in the world.

GLOBAL WAR, 1939–1945

Every army that had experienced the trench stalemate of World War I had learned a hard lesson from sniper activity, yet at the outbreak of war in 1939 it appeared that once again history had been ignored. Britain had curtailed training, reducing its sniper complement to eight men per battalion, and in 1921 existing stocks of scope-equipped Mk III SMLEs were broken up, the scopes being sold off for commercial use. The United States Army had no official sniper training programme, and only a small number of dedicated Marine snipers. France and Italy had no trained snipers at all, and during the Weimar period even Germany all but dismissed the sniper as tactically irrelevant. In a memorandum from the German Chief of Army Command dated 5 December 1931 it was recommended that 'Telescopic sight carbines should be used up. Parts for mounting the telescopic sight as well as spare parts … will no longer be kept in stock. Telescopic sight carbines in need of repair will be exchanged for rifles.' In short, once worn out the snipers' rifles were not to be replaced and no more snipers were to be trained. Of the major powers, only Russia recognised the value of trained snipers. Yet by 1942 all of the combatant nations were once again fielding such specialists. What happened to change the minds of the military?

The answer lay in the realisation during the 1930s that the spectre of war was again looming over Europe and that sniping had not simply been an isolated phenomenon of the trench war 20 years before. Germany ceased selling off its scoped rifles; and under the orders of Heinrich Himmler – an avid exponent of sniping – the Waffen-SS began a sniper training programme. Germany was as short of good sniping rifles as any other country, for little postwar weapons development had been undertaken. There had been some slight improvements in telescopic sights due to German manufacturers' efforts to improve the magnification power of scopes during the interwar period. A new breed of more compact 4x and 6x power scopes was being produced, which gave a sniper the theoretical ability to register hits out to 800 metres.

Russian M1891/30 Moisin-Nagant with PU scope. Particularly accurate rifles were selected from production lines and mated to a telescopic sight. The simple adjusting drums on the scope and the large trigger guard were designed to be used with gloved fingers. (Courtesy Geoffrey Brown)

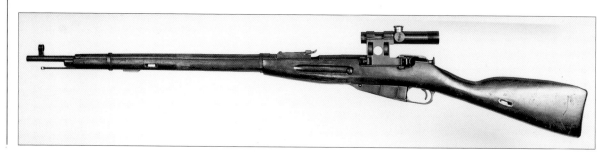

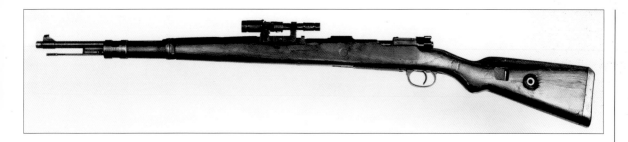

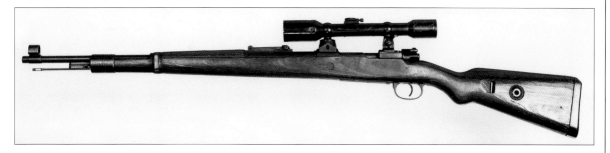

However, for most of World War II sniping scopes were largely to remain 3x or 4x power. There were also some improvements in lens design, enhancing the performance of scopes at low light levels and thus giving a sniper a far better chance of picking out and hitting a target at times when the unwary believed themselves to be invisible. However, as the *Blitzkreig* rolled across Europe in 1939-40 there seemed little apparent need for snipers. Initially the Germans faced little opposition apart from ill-equipped French and Polish snipers who, though valiant, were woefully few in number and could do little to stem the invading flood. The first real proof of the power of the sniper was to become evident during the German invasion of Russia in 1941.

Snipers on the Eastern Front

Russian doctrine for sniper training took a rather broader view than that of other nations. The Russians claimed that by 1938 six million soldiers had qualified for the 'Voroshiloff Sharpshooter' badge. This is not to say that these men were true snipers, but they were trained riflemen who gave the Russian command a very deep pool when it came to selecting snipers. Some indication of how seriously the Soviet High Command took sniping is the fact that over 53,000 Moisin-Nagant sniping rifles were manufactured up to 1938; by 1942 the same number were being manufactured *annually*.

In practice, wartime Soviet snipers were probably less well trained than their counterparts in other armies, as the need to put them into the field at once and in large numbers overrode all other considerations. During the heavy fighting on the Eastern Front an experienced sniper would be allocated a couple of neophyte snipers who, if they were lucky, received two weeks' front line training before they were left to fend for themselves. The Red Army publicity machine enthusiastically promoted the new cult of 'sniperism', but not everyone believed spectacular Soviet claims about their sniping. Captain Charles Shore, a British sniper officer who wrote an informed and critical book on wartime sniping, stated: 'Summing up … about Russian snipers and sniper training, it

TOP **The German 7.92mm K98k equipped with the tiny 1.5x power Z41 scope. The extremely long eye relief can be seen when compared with the turret-mount K98k. Although never designed as a primary sniping sight, some 87,400 Z41s were manufactured, more than any other German telescopic sight. (Courtesy Geoffrey Brown)**

ABOVE **Arguably the best sniping rifle produced by Germany – the K98k with a 3x power high turret-mount scope. The elevation drum is visible on top of the scope body; windage was compensated for by means of an adjuster screw on the right side of the rear mount. (Courtesy Geoffrey Brown)**

would appear that it [sniping] is not as we know it, but suggests rather close quarter fighting and maybe sharpshooting in its lowest form.'

This dismissive verdict is probably unjust, as it was already proven that to be effective a sniper did not necessarily need to be shooting at long range with a scoped rifle. The Russians had very large numbers of competent riflemen who were able to shoot very accurately at ranges of up to 400 metres, lending credence to the myth that every other Russian soldier was a sniper. They were not – but it may have felt like that to the Germans. The Russians certainly did have some very talented snipers; and there is clear evidence that the volume and effect of Soviet marksmanship seriously worried the Germans, to the extent that they adopted a training programme for their own snipers based upon that used by the Russians.

Some indication of the losses inflicted by the Russians can be glimpsed from one assault by the German 465th Infantry Regiment in September 1941 on a thickly wooded area. In a few hours they lost 75 dead and 25 missing to what were described as 'tree snipers' who melted away as the Germans advanced. The Russians proved to be bitterly stubborn adversaries, well equipped and fanatical in their desire to wreak revenge on the invaders. One German account tells of a single sniper who steadily inflicted casualties on a resting Panzer unit over a five-day period. All attempts to locate him failed. One morning a sharp-eyed German observer saw in the bright cold sunlight what appeared to be smoke coming from a knocked out Russian T34 tank. Investigation showed it to be the breath of a sniper, who had been living in the tank amongst its dead crew for nearly a week. He had survived by eating the crew's frozen rations and by thawing out their waterbottles under his clothing. There is no record of his fate, but it was doubtless swiftly and ruthlessly administered.

The standard Russian sniping rifle was the Moisin-Nagant 91/30, originally equipped with a 4x PT telescopic sight made by Carl Zeiss, a company that Russia had purchased in the 1930s. When supplies of the PT dried up in 1935 the Soviets copied it, calling it the VP or PEM; but from 1940 these began to be replaced by the smaller, lighter 3.5x PU, although all three were in use throughout the war. The veteran Moisin could achieve good accuracy out to 800 metres, but as the war progressed quality varied greatly; some captured examples that were tested were reckoned to be of use only out to 400 yards or so. This was not a great handicap, as much street sniping was done at short ranges, but in open warfare on the vast steppes an accurate rifle was invaluable. The Russians also took the lead in introducing a gas-operated semi-automatic sniping rifle, the M1938 Tokarev, a mechanism that they were to retain on their sniping rifles to the present day.

German 7.92mm Karabiner 43/ZF4 combination. Germany had high hopes for this semi-automatic rifle, but it did not meet expectations. Although the compact 4x power scopes were excellent, production problems meant that weapons suffered from variable accuracy and some serious component failures. (Courtesy Geoffrey Brown)

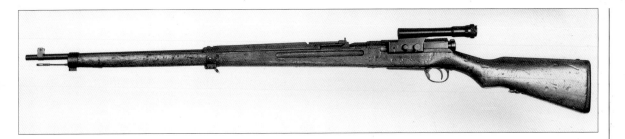

Initially the Germans had little or no means of combating the Russians. There were some Heer and Waffen-SS snipers, but rifles were in short supply, the Germans frequently resorting to using Moisins captured from the Polish and Soviet armies. The demand for men to train as snipers meant that an above average shot in an infantry unit could find himself ordered from the front line to attend a sniping school. There he would be issued with a matched rifle and scope with which he would train and fight for the rest of his service career. The weapons varied from Great War vintage Gewehr 98s fitted with early commercial scopes, to the issue Mauser K98k mated to a 3x or 4x power telescopic sight produced by any one of a dozen manufacturers. As the war progressed different services trained their own snipers, so that Luftwaffe Fallschmirmjäger, Waffen-SS and Heer snipers were all fielded. As a result, by 1944 there were no less than 30 German sniper training schools in existence, and the German sniper had the greatest choice of telescope-equipped rifles of any nation, with some ten standard models plus a host of variants.

Sniping in the Pacific

Meanwhile the Americans were facing an unexpected adversary in very different terrain. Prewar US Army interest in sniping had been virtually non-existent, the training school at Camp Perry providing only a brief course with almost no practical field training. The Army snipers were equipped with the .30 calibre M1903 A-3 and A-4 Springfield sniping rifle adopted in 1942 and fitted with a commercial 2.5x Weaver 330 scope, designated the M73B1. This scope, although adequate for its original purpose of deer-hunting, proved rather fragile when subjected to the rigours of field use in the Pacific; and as the rifle had no 'iron' sights fitted, damaging the scope rendered the weapon useless. However, the Springfields were issued in considerable quantities, some 28,000 being manufactured, and the type remained in service throughout the war despite its shortcomings.

Japanese 6.5mm Type 97 sniping rifle. These were fitted with either a 2.5x or 4x power scope; this example is the 2.5x power, with a 10 degree field of view. These scopes have no provision for windage or elevation adjustment; instead the reticule is graduated to allow the sniper to compensate visually. (Courtesy Geoffrey Brown)

US Marine snipers in action on Okinawa in May 1945. Both are using .30cal M1903 Springfields equipped with Unertl scopes. These commercial scopes were normally fitted with a spring buffer as a recoil absorber, but these were omitted from military scopes to prevent sand or dirt jamming between the tube and mounts; most Marines used a piece of rubber inner tube to pull the scope back into position after each shot. (Courtesy US National Archives, Marine Corps Collection)

From late 1944 specially accurised semi-automatic .30 calibre Garand M1 rifles mated to a military version of the robust 2.2x power Lyman Alaskan scope began to be issued in small numbers, the combination being known as the M1C. Although developed too late in the war to have any real impact, the pairing was to prove a good combination. Some 6,700 were produced, and many M1C and M1D

British observer using a 20x power telescope, its leather carrying case lying next to it; though slightly unwieldy, this was excellent for target spotting. It was not until the Vietnam War that the use of telescopes became more common among scout-snipers, the 20x power M49 increasingly being adopted by the US in place of the standard issue 7x50 binoculars. (Crown copyright)

variants would eventually see service in Korea and Vietnam with both the Army and Marines.

The Marine Corps had always taken a very positive view of sniping and actively encouraged target shooting. Good marksmen were selected from units and trained in scouting and sniping on an informal basis until December 1942, when a Corps sniping school was opened at Fort Bragg. They were mainly equipped with '03 Springfields, but unlike the Army rifles these were mated to the distinctive Unertl scope attached to the rifle with special duralium mounts. It was a potent combination, providing target magnification out to ranges unattainable by the standard issue Weaver or Lyman scopes. In capable hands it was possible to shoot accurately to over 1,000 yards – as Pte David Cass proved on Okinawa in 1945, when he shot the crew of a Japanese machine gun at a range of 1,200 yards. The Leathernecks also broke with tradition in using some commercial hunting rifles, heavy-barrelled Winchester Model 70s mated to the Unertl scope. Although this combination was officially rejected as an issue sniping rifle some continued in service, and the Marines' use of commercial target rifles was to set a precedent for later wars.

In the Pacific islands and the jungles of Burma and New Guinea the Allied snipers had a difficult task. The dense tropical canopy and undergrowth meant that the need was for quick reflexes and maximum firepower rather than long-range accuracy, a problem that was to re-emerge some 20 years later in Vietnam. With combat ranges typically under 50 yards and sometimes point-blank, there was little opportunity for the snipers to test their skills to the limit. The Allied soldiers learned very quickly that Japanese snipers were masters of camouflage, with trees and 'spider holes' being favourite sniping positions. The Japanese would often wait until their intended target had walked past before opening fire with a rifle or even a light machine gun. From the viewpoint of concealment, a tree was probably the worst possible place for a sniper to choose as it was only a matter of time before he was located, and once that happened he was a sitting duck. K.W.Cooper, an officer of the 2nd Bn The Border Regiment with British 14th Army in Burma, used the firepower of the Bren gun as an effective counter-sniper weapon:

'I thought I saw movement in the branches of one of the higher trees. Squirming behind the Bren … I suddenly saw the unmistakable flash of an automatic weapon. Taking aim I loosed off practically a whole magazine into the tree and was rather surprised to see something thresh down out of the branches and begin to swing like a pendulum above the roof of a burning hut. "You got the sod. He's on the end of a bloody rope" – Smith was jubilant as he leaned across to slap another magazine down beside the gun.'

This vulnerability did not appear to worry the Japanese, who exacted a heavy toll. In the Pacific, infantry companies suffered heavy casualty levels as a result of sniper fire from the treeline that fringed most islands. First Sergeant Fusco of the US 27th Infantry Division fought on Makin Island in late 1943, and recounted shortly afterwards how his men dealt with the tree snipers: 'Smoking out the snipers that were in the trees was the worst part of it. We couldn't spot them even with glasses and it made our advance very slow. When we moved forward it was as a skirmish line … if one of our men began to fire rapidly into a tree or ground location, we knew that he had spotted a sniper, and those who could see took up the fire. When we saw no enemy we fired occasional shots into trees that looked likely.'

The British and Commonwealth troops preferred planned counter-sniping whenever possible. A number of methods were adopted, but the most effective was the use of organised groups of counter-sniper teams. Indeed, when two Commonwealth brigades combined their sniper teams in Burma and fielded 48 men, they were able to inflict 296 casualties on the Japanese for the loss of only two of their own snipers.

The Japanese were equipped with a number of different types of rifles, the earliest, a 6.5mm Type 38, dating back to 1905. Under the guidance of Col Namio Tatsumi, the 6.5mm Type 97 and 7.7mm Type 99 rifles were developed, being equipped with 2.5x or 4x power telescopic sights. One advantage of the smaller 6.5mm cartridge was that there was almost no smoke from the discharge, and the sound of the rifle – a distinctive high-pitched 'crack' – made it very difficult to locate. Although the Japanese had adequate supplies of sniping rifles, much of their shooting was done at comparatively close range using a wide variety of weapons and open sights. Well equipped and suicidally determined, the Japanese frequently fought the Allies to a standstill, earning the grudging admiration of those who faced them.

British snipers

In 1939 Britain was still equipped with the Great War vintage P1914 Mk I (T) sniping rifle, but fortunately the Army possessed a number of officers and men of some vision who were determined to see sniping reinstated. The authorities reacted with remarkable speed, and by 1940 a training school had been set up at Bisley, to be followed by schools in Wales and Scotland. The Lovat Scouts were again employed to teach their unique stalking and camouflage skills, and an extended three-week course saw qualified snipers being returned to their units. Although sterling work was done by snipers in France and Norway in 1940-41, the early war years gave British and Commonwealth snipers little chance for action. The vast distances, lack of cover, and heat distortion in the Western Desert were not conducive to sniping, and it was not until they reached Sicily and Italy in mid-1943 that snipers began to prove their worth. One

The British .303in Enfield No.4 Mk I (T) rifle, the standard sniping rifle for the British Army for almost 30 years. The telescopic sight was quickly detachable by means of two large thumbscrews and came with a substantial steel carrying case. The wooden cheekpiece was factory-fitted and brought the shooter's eye into line with the scope. (Courtesy Geoffrey Brown)

of the great advantages that British snipers enjoyed was in retaining the Great War period scout telescope, an instrument which – inexplicably – no other army had adopted. One British sniping officer in Italy went so far as to say that the 14 telescopes in the battalion were 'the best weapons they had', and that his men could 'see miles farther than the Hun could, and that certainly gave one confidence, especially when out sniping.'

In 1942 a new rifle was adopted to replace the aged P14, the Enfield No.4 Mk I (T). This was a standard No.4, selected from the production line and sent to Holland & Holland in London, where it was carefully rebuilt by hand, ensuring that the barrel was properly bedded and the scope and bore were perfectly aligned. It was given a set of machined steel mounting blocks to which were fitted a cast iron mount and a 3x power No.32 Mk I telescopic sight. Although criticised for the fragility of its elevation and windage adjustment system, the No.32 proved a very durable scope and in modified form was to remain in service until 1970. Despite some teething troubles the new rifle proved very popular and particularly accurate at longer ranges. A British sniper in Italy, working with two American observers, spotted a group of Germans at 700 yards' range and, to the disbelief of the Yanks, suggested 'having a crack at them' with his No.4 (T). He scored several hits and reported with satisfaction on 'the expression of utter surprise on [the Germans'] faces at being sniped at. [Their] attitude after this bout of long range sniping was not half so cocksure and brazen.'

Ranges, ammunition and camouflage

Although under favourable circumstances long-range sniping was certainly possible, particularly if a 6x power scope was available, in practice the use of ordinary production military rifles allied to the relatively low power of most telescopic sights meant that true long-range shooting – i.e. at ranges of over 600 yards – was rare. Although most military scopes were graduated up to 1,200 yards/metres or beyond, experience showed that attempting to shoot out to these ranges was generally a waste of time. Captain Shore had an interesting comment on the level of accuracy expected from service sniping rifles. He said that 'a man who is capable of consistently (every time he shoots) putting up five shot 2 inch groups at 100 yards with a service rifle equipped with a telescopic sight is a superb shot'. This is really not much of an improvement over the performance of Great War rifles, but unsurprising considering that most

OPPOSITE **The shortage of sniping rifles led Australia to adopt its own in 1944 in the form of the Rifle No.1 MkIII* HT. These utilised Lithgow-produced actions mated to Pattern 1918 scopes, on either high or low mounts. The rifle proved quite successful and some saw use during the Korean War. (Courtesy Geoffrey Brown)**

A British sniper armed with a No.4 Mk I (T) and his observer with spotting scope undergo sniper training in the Middle East. They wear one-piece overalls camouflaged with paint and camouflage netting over their heads, the rifle and scope also being carefully wrapped; sandbags cover their black boots. (Courtesy Imperial War Museum, neg.E30306)

service weapons were little changed from those of a generation before. Matthias Hertzenauer, one of the most skilled of German snipers, reckoned that with a K98k he could shoot out to a maximum 700-800 metres and achieve a 400 metre head or 600 metre body hit, but only if he was using a 6x power scope. While this certainly appears an improvement over hit probability ranges for the 1914-18 period, it should be borne in mind that Hertzenaur was an extraordinarily gifted shot.

Where ammunition was concerned Germany alone had appreciated that special supplies were required for snipers. In a report dated July 1944 the problem of supplying high-grade match quality ammunition was examined: 'The normal Sm.E. [ball] ammunition allows no precision shooting over 300-400 metres, as must be demanded of sharpshooters at these and greater ranges. Until now it was possible to equip the sharpshooter with select s.S. ammunition which at the present time is only available in small quantities, or not at all. The General of Infantry therefore demands the production of suitable sharpshooter ammunition at a volume of 20 million cartridges monthly.' By 1945 special s.S. ammunition was available in quantity to most German snipers, but no other country had supplies of special sniping ammunition. Britain regarded the quality control on their Mk VII cartridge as sufficiently high for sniping use, although most snipers had a preference for one make of cartridge over another. Captain Shore noted that he 'used a great deal of American .303 (particularly WRA) and this gave consistently finer shooting' – WRA being Winchester Repeating Arms. Many American snipers who had been experienced peacetime shooters appreciated the accuracy of match-quality ammunition and when possible had supplies sent to them from home.

By the time the Allies invaded Normandy sniping on both sides had developed into a deadly serious business. The Germans were able to field large numbers of very experienced snipers, such as Sepp Allenberger and Matthias Hertzenauer who between them had accounted for over 600 Russians. Such men had learned all the tricks of the trade on the Eastern Front and they proved formidable adversaries, picking off officers and NCOs with depressing ease. One captured German sniper, when quizzed as to how he was able to pick out officers who wore ordinary battledress, carried rifles and wore no rank badges, said simply 'We shoot the men who have moustaches' – they had appreciated that in the British and US armies facial hair was usually the prerogative of officers and senior NCOs.

Special clothing was by this time routinely used by snipers of both sides, each man wearing what was practical, comfortable and readily to hand. Special insignia were conspicuous by their absence; snipers knew that their chances of survival if captured and identified were slim, and wore whatever would give them a sporting chance of passing themselves off as ordinary infantrymen in the confusion of battle. The use of the sniper in the more mobile warfare of World War II meant that a light fighting order was adopted by most armies. Aside from his rifle and clothing, a British sniper in NW Europe in 1944-45 might carry a tobacco tin containing spare parts for his rifle, binoculars, a compass, a couple of No. 36 hand grenades, a couple of camouflaged face veils, 50 rounds of ball ammunition in a bandolier and five each of tracer and

Canada modified the issue Enfield No.4 Mk I (T) by fitting a sporting type stock with cheekrest and a rubber recoil pad; a Canadian-made REL C No.67 Mk I telescopic sight was mounted on a quick-release rail. (Courtesy Geoffrey Brown)

armour-piercing; his waterbottle, boiled sweets (hard candy) and as much chocolate as he could lay his hands on.

The demands made on snipers were varied: penetrating enemy lines prior to an attack, targeting officers, artillerymen and machine gun crews, or providing delaying action in the event of a retreat, thus preventing enemy advance units from deploying effectively. There was no such thing as an average day. Arthur Hare, a native of Cambridge, joined up as a prewar Regular soldier, becoming a corporal sniper and serving with the advancing British Army through Belgium, Holland and Germany. In a book he outlined some of his sniping duties, which included acting as an advance observer for a 25-pounder artillery battery, fighting as an infantryman to beat off a counter-attack, street fighting in Holland and Germany, and countless hours of lying silently in foxholes with a radio set doing nothing but using his powers of observation.

Hare detailed the start of a day that was to prove productive. It began with orders to proceed with three other snipers to a distant farmhouse prior to an assault across a river by British troops. A cold, dark, predawn start saw the grumbling snipers installed in various parts of the house where they lay motionless until 2.30 in the afternoon, when suddenly British shells began landing on the German positions 150 yards away. As his companions opened fire, Hare immediately shot down the sentry on the bridge, before swinging his aim to the door of a farmhouse across the river which flew open. A bareheaded German officer rushed out, making a few yards before Hare's shot knocked him down. Hare chambered another round as a second man ran out. 'Again the bullet smashed home, the unfortunate recipient seeming to leap high in the air. The third man made twenty yards … he slumped to the ground tearing at his throat. This time two Germans ran out, so that the fifth man got away.' The small group of snipers kept doggedly shooting, despite shells dropping on their house, and in ten minutes the battle was over. As British forces moved towards the bridgehead Hare observed the Germans who had been their targets, ' … still in their position surrounding the bridge; but they made no movement and fired no guns. Their faces were waxy, eyes staring, some with triumphant grins, others frozen for all time … fear, anger, despair showed plainly on their features. Some old, some young, all battle weary and now hardly even human. Gradually the sound of battle subsided, the smoke drifted away …'.

After eight stiff, cold, dull hours in the same position, the snipers saw ten minutes of frantic action, accounting for some 200 dead, wounded and captured. The dirty, unshaven, exhausted men trudged back to their billets, where the battalion CO ordered a stiff issue of rum for each man. Normally cool, Hare was surprised to find that he had developed the shakes. He was even more astonished to be awarded the Military Medal for his part in the attack.

By 1945 sniping had proved its worth countless times on every battlefront. There was little doubt in the minds of those who had fought as front line soldiers as to the sniper's efficiency not only in killing, but in gathering vital intelligence information, as well as spreading confusion and demoralisation among the enemy. Yet within months of the war ending the snipers were demobilised or returned to their units as ordinary riflemen, and their hard-learned skills evaporated like mist on a hot day.

1: Captain, Gloucestershire Regt, BEF; Flanders, 1915
2: Scout-sniper, Arras, 1917
3: Sergeant observer, KRRC, 41st Div, 1917

A

1: Sniper team, Jäger-Bataillon Nr.8;
   Alsace, spring 1915
2: Scharfschütze, France 1918

B

1: Sniper, Japanese SNLF; Pacific, 1943-45
2 & 3: US Army sniper team, Pacific, 1944-45

C

1: Female sniper, Red Army, 1943
2: Sniper, Red Army, 1944-45

1

2

1: Sniper, 2.FJD;
   Dutch/German border,
   winter 1944
2: Sniper,
   6.SS-Gebirgs-Div
   'Nord'; Russia, 1943

E

2

1

1 & 2: British sniper team, NW Europe, autumn 1944

F

1: Sniper, Royal Australian Regt; Korea, summer 1952
2: Counter-sniper, British 22nd SAS Regt; Oman, early 1970s

1 & 2: Sniper team, US 5th Marines; South Vietnam, 1970

1: Sniper, British Parachute Regt; Falklands, 1982
2: Sniper, Argentine Regimiento (Especial) de Infanteria 25;
   Islas Malvinas, 1982

1

2

1: Sniper, Soviet 103rd Guards
   Air Assault Div;
   Afghanistan, 1985
2: Sniper, 2e REI,
   French Foreign Legion;
   Bosnia, winter 1995

1

2

J

1: Sniper, US Army Special Forces, Gulf War, 1990-91
2 & 3: US Marine sniper team, Gulf War, 1991

K

Sniping positions, France, 1944 – see commentary for details

1945 – THE OUTBREAK OF 'PEACE'

There have been more wars since 1945 than there were in the entire century before it; and while none have been truly global in nature, many – such as the Korean, Vietnamese and recent Balkan wars – have involved large multi-national forces. After 1945 there was clearly no requirement to maintain wartime levels of defence expenditure; civilian populations were heartily sick of war and all the privations that went with it, and in such a climate defence spending was cut drastically. Snipers, a necessity in wartime, became an expendable peacetime luxury, and sniper training virtually ceased. As early as May 1945 even the US Marines – the keepers of the flame – had formulated a schedule for the disposal of surplus Springfield sniping rifles.

Despite the technical improvements of the late war years, no significant postwar military development work was undertaken on rifles or telescopic sights. When war broke out in Korea in June 1950 military interest in sniping was briefly rekindled, mainly due to the very effective level of Communist sniping. The North Koreans used a wide variety of rifles – Russian, Chinese, and even Remington '03s supplied to Nationalist China during World War II. They had a good sniper training programme and were tough and determined adversaries, and it took very little time for newly arrived US units to appreciate what they were up against. On his first day in the line the commander of the 3rd Bn, 1st US Marines was viewing the Korean positions when a sniper's bullet smashed the binoculars out of his hands. Astonished that there were no official sniper units to call on, he ordered his gunnery sergeant to select the best shots in the battalion and train them. Old 1903-A4 Springfields and Garand M1Ds were requisitioned and an impromptu snipers' course was organised. Other field commanders quickly realised the same need, and both Britain and Australia hurriedly introduced sniping courses, issuing the trusty Enfield No.4 Mk I (T) and old P14 No.3 Mk I (T) rifles to their men. That these counter-sniper measures proved effective was in no doubt, as within weeks men were able to walk openly along their lines safe from aimed enemy fire. In an interesting parallel to the war of 1914-18, the use of snipers in Korea was generally regarded by the Western powers as purely a wartime expedient, with no official long-term training programme being devised. However, the United States and Great Britain were becoming aware that their sniping rifles were at the end of their useful design lives and both were looking to find replacements.

There had been a major shift in weapon design during World War II, with the adoption of semi-automatics for the infantry by the United States, Russia and Germany. Experience with

A British sniper in Aden, 1964. He has a No.4 (T) rifle and – unusually – carries his ammunition in an open-looped leather belt. The canvas carrying case for the No.32 scope hangs at his side. His rifle and equipment vary little from those used during World War I. (Crown copyright)

45

semi-automatic sniping rifles had proven that a sniper could aim and fire faster than with a bolt action. The act of firing initially causes a loss of sight picture as the rifle recoils, added to which is the need to work the bolt mechanism to eject the spent case and chamber a new round. The time spent doing this almost invariably meant that the chances of firing a second shot would be lost as the target immediately took cover. The Germans had put considerable effort into developing a purpose-designed sniper variant of the Karabiner 43; the Selbstladegewehr 43 was a gas-operated semi-automatic weapon, but it proved to have only average performance and was mechanically unreliable. In practice many snipers disliked semi-automatics as they were both heavier than a bolt action, more prone to malfunction, and less accurate at long range. However, in 1957 America introduced the M14, an improved version of the M1 Garand. It was chambered for the new 7.62mm military cartridge and fitted with a fire selector enabling a rapid change from semi-automatic to full automatic mode. Curiously, although the new weapons were manufactured with a groove and screw recess on the left side to accept a scope mount, no mount was actually produced.

An American sniper of the 45th Infantry Division lies in wait near 'Ice Cream Cone Hill' in Korea, November 1952. He has sacking wrapped around his helmet to soften its silhouette. The intense winter cold in Korea was a problem for snipers, who had to wear impractically heavy clothing and gloves to protect against frostbite. (Courtesy US Army Military History Institute)

Vietnam

The conflict that erupted in South Vietnam in the mid-1960s was to prove something of a watershed for sniping, in terms of both technology and tactics. War had been rumbling on in the former French Indochina since the late 1940s. Faced with the threat of Communism running riot in South-East Asia, America entered the war in strength in 1965. Once again history was destined to repeat itself, for with the deployment of the first combat units came the realisation that not a single man arrived trained as a sniper. In addition both the Viet Cong and North Vietnamese Army were fielding snipers; and the standard M14 with iron sights proved inadequate for shooting beyond about 500 metres. The problem was further compounded in 1966 when the M14 began to be replaced by the M16 in .223in calibre (5.56mm). Its tiny, high velocity bullet performed well out to 300 metres but it was certainly not a long-range sniping weapon.

In desperation, a few men had commercial scopes mailed to them and persuaded unit armourers fit them to M16s, with some success. One officer in the 25th Infantry Division had an impressive tally of 50 kills with a scoped M16 by the time he was shipped home in late 1966. The Army had largely ignored the sniper question until, through the efforts of Gen Julian Ewell, a sniping policy was devised for the 9th Infantry Division that began to achieve results. He assigned two snipers to each brigade HQ and six per battalion, to work with patrols and also take on designated targets.

Development work also began in earnest on finding a suitable rifle and scope for the US Army. Most testing was done in the field, and the Winchester Model 70, Remington 700, M16 and M14 were trialled. A match-grade M14 equipped with a Redfield 3x/9x ART (Auto Ranging Telescope) was judged the most suitable, the combination being given the designation XM21. Some M14's were also fitted with vintage M84 scopes, which worked quite effectively. Interestingly, and at odds with the Marines' view of their Remingtons, a survey undertaken among Army snipers showed that 85 per cent of them preferred the

A sniper of the US 3rd Marine Division in Vietnam uses a seated position to brace his Model 70 Winchester. Although this was replaced by the 7.62mm Model 700 Remington, many Marine snipers felt that the old .30-06 cartridge used in the Winchester made it a better long-range rifle. The extreme length of the 8x power Unertl telescope can be clearly seen, as can the thickness of the heavy barrel. (Courtesy US National Archives, Marine Corps Collection)

M14 to the bolt action Winchester, and all questioned were in agreement that the M14/M84 combination was the best sniping rifle for the purpose. A great advantage for Army snipers using the M14 was that it could be equipped with a Starlight night vision device, which gave a green image sharp enough to permit shooting out to 400 metres. About 15 per cent of night operation kills were due to the Starlight; however, issue was limited, they were heavy at 5lbs (2.2kg), delicate and very expensive.

The Marines had tackled the sniping problem with typically direct action. Under the direction of Maj Robert Russell a number of Winchester Model 70s chambered for commercial .30-06 ammunition were acquired and mated with the Unertl scope of World War II vintage. It proved a good marriage, allowing the Marines to outshoot enemy snipers and to carry the war well beyond the confines of the front lines, such as they were. However, they calculated that they would require a minimum of 550 sniping rifles for training and combat, plus replacements for service-damaged weapons; they needed a rifle that could be supplied in quantity. It had to be chambered for 7.62mm ammunition, be simple, accurate to 1,000 yards, and have a telescopic sight capable of withstanding fearsome levels of humidity – often 100 per cent in temperatures in excess of 100° Fahrenheit. Of those tested they selected the heavy-barrelled Remington 700 also equipped with a Redfield 3x/9x ART scope. Some 1,000 Model 700s were supplied by Remington during the conflict, designated the Model 40. Used with Lake City Arsenal-manufactured M118 Match Grade ammunition the Remingtons proved excellent weapons, capable of very long-range shooting, although it sometimes took extraordinary perseverance to achieve results, as Sgt Ed Kugler of the 4th Marines recalled. He spotted a Viet Cong soldier at extreme range:

'It looked on the map to be about thirteen hundred metres. What a shot that would be. I dialled my scope [magnification] to the max of nine power. He was damned tiny at thirteen hundred yards.' Kugler fired a full magazine of five rounds without scoring a hit, although he forced the VC to take cover. He refused to give up, sure that his target would reappear, which he did two hours later. 'It was nearing 1700 hours and I knew the game would end soon. I aimed so high his head was in the bottom half of the vertical crosshair. My rifle had to be sticking up in the air like a mortar! I relaxed, held back on that stock, breathed as right as I ever had and BOOM! He fell like a rock. It had taken me six shots, but hell, if he was stupid enough to stay in sight that was his problem.'

The Marines believed that their bolt action rifles were superior in accuracy and reliability to semi-automatics, but there were shortcomings. The ability of a semi-automatic to deliver rapid fire meant that in close-quarter jungle firefights the M14 with its 20-round magazine was in many respects a more practical weapon than the five-shot bolt action Remington. Many snipers compromised by carrying both, as Sgt Kugler acknowledged: 'Zulu and I both had M14s. The problem was we had to carry them and our sniper rifles. It was tough trying to walk through a jungle with a big barrel sticking up to catch onto everything. On the other hand it was pretty fruitless to carry a weapon that could shoot for a thousand yards in a jungle where I couldn't see twenty feet.'

While the US held complete air superiority and had overwhelming artillery power, the dominance of terrain established by their ground troops was limited, particularly at night. Initially snipers accompanied infantry patrols, where they were vulnerable to ambush and booby traps and their effectiveness was hampered by the thick jungle. As probably no more than 1,000-1,200 snipers served in Vietnam during the entire conflict, the use of these highly skilled men on patrols was clearly wasteful; increasingly they were given free rein to conduct search-and-kill missions, which they did with determination. Gradually this policy began to pay dividends, becoming so effective that the North Vietnamese placed a bounty on the head of any American captured carrying a 'long rifle'.

As in previous wars, the usefulness of snipers was not always accepted unquestioningly by many infantrymen, who were prone to a sense of unease when the snipers were around, and who regarded them as *prima donnas* who didn't share the same hardships of fatigues and living conditions. An Army sniper recalled that when he entered a dugout one infantry private nudged another and whispered, 'Uh-oh, here comes Murder Incorporated'. On the other hand, possession of a sniping rifle was an open passport to almost anywhere in front of or behind the lines. Nobody much cared to enquire too deeply what a sniper was doing, or why.

The British 7.62mm L42 rifle with No.32 Mk III (L1A1) scope. Curiously, the L42 was almost a pound heavier, at 12lbs 6oz (5.6kg), than the No.4 (T) which it replaced. This was mainly due to the more accurate heavy target barrel fitted. In other respects it was little different from the old Enfield. (Courtesy Geoffrey Brown)

The British Commonwealth and Russia

Elsewhere, other countries had been embroiled in smaller wars. British involvement in Aden in the mid-1960s and Oman in the first half of the 1970s had prompted the use of SAS and Royal Marine Commando sniper teams to combat Arab guerrillas, at times with a little unconventional help. In Aden in 1967 a troublesome sniper well hidden in a house defied attempts by 42 Commando RM snipers to silence him, so they used a Carl Gustav anti-tank rocket launcher to settle the problem. The venerable No.4 Mk I (T) was still the issue sniping rifle, although Britain and the Dominions realised that it had outlived its useful life. The British Army had re-equipped with the 7.62mm L1A1 Self-Loading Rifle in the late 1950s, which did not lend itself to effective modification for sniping, but finding yet another rifle for limited issue to snipers was not seen as a priority. A committee was formed to investigate replacing the No.4, and eventually a compromise was reached with the production of the L42A1 – effectively a No.4 Mk I (T) converted to 7.62mm and fitted with a heavyweight target barrel. It retained the old 3x power No.32 Mk III scope, redesignated the L1A1. However, both Australia and Canada chose a different route, adopting a purpose-built sniping rifle – the Parker Hale 1200 TX, equipped with a 6x power Kahles telescopic sight. They were the first Western armies to reject modified service rifles in favour of a purpose-designed weapon for military sniping, and they set a trend that has since been followed by the majority of other Western military powers.

Falkland Islands, 1982: an infantryman from 2nd Bn, Scots Guards watches over Argentinian prisoners. His L1A1 SLR has the bulky AN/PVS-2 night sight fitted. Although the SLR did not lend itself to sniping, it was very effective out to 400 yards with this night sight, and both sides made good use of these devices. (Courtesy HQ Land Command)

The L42 saw some hard use in the intervening years, in the Middle East, Northern Ireland and during the Falklands campaign, where it did not always cope well with the harsh climate. Scopes fogged up, the adjusting drums were troublesome, and some snipers had problems with the functioning of the bolt mechanism. One infantry sniper told the author that his L42 jammed so frequently that he heaved it into a stream in a fit of pique, picked up an Argentinian FN SLR, and happily used it for the rest of the campaign, during which it functioned faultlessly. Clearly Britain urgently needed to find a

replacement for the L42; and in 1982 five rifles were tested against a stringent set of requirements. The winner was the PM rifle, made by Accuracy International and subsequently adopted into service as the L96A1. It was equipped with a 6x42 or 10x56 Schmidt & Bender scope and chambered for the standard 7.62mm NATO cartridge. Some indication of the level of accuracy that specially designed rifles such as the L96 can achieve is that snipers now expect to attain one-shot head hits at 800 metres.

If the West was beginning to look towards military variants of sporting target rifles, what of sniper weapons development elsewhere? Eastern Bloc countries followed the path of development taken by the Russians, who had long believed in the advantages of the semi-automatic rifle. Their adoption of the AK47 assault rifle as the standard service weapon after 1946 led to the introduction of the Dragunov SVD in the mid-1960s. This was a purpose designed semi-automatic sniping rifle based around the mechanism of the AK, but using the old, powerful, rimmed 7.62x54mm cartridge. It would accept any Russian military telescopic sight, but was generally equipped with the excellent PSO1. Many other countries, such as Yugoslavia, Czechoslovakia, Israel and Germany, adopted the SVD or variants. There were disadvantages in the semi-automatic mechanism; in Vietnam, one American sniper recalled that he detected the positions of more enemy snipers through the sun glinting on the brass cases ejecting from AKs than by any other means. They are invariably heavy, making freehand shooting very difficult – e.g. the Israeli Galil, loaded and with its bipod, weighs an impressive 14.1lbs (6.4kg) – but given a solid shooting platform they can perform impressively. In an interview shortly after the event Chuck Kramer, a

sniper training adviser to the Israelis, recalled using one on a moving target during the fighting against the PLO in Beirut in 1982:

'Most of the kills were made at 600-800 metres … I saw this big motor scooter coming towards me about a kilometre away with two guys on it. They're both carrying SKS carbines … and these canvas carriers for the RPGs on the front of the motor scooter. I lined them up … by sheer instinct. It was a classic shot. The round must have gone through the driver and then into the passenger.'

Private Rawstron of the 1st Bn, Parachute Regiment rests during a patrol in Pristina, Kosovo, summer 1999. He carries a field-camouflaged 7.62mm L96 rifle, now adopted by the British Army as their frontline sniping weapon. He is being guarded by a poorly armed but very determined looking local boy. (Courtesy HQ Land Command)

The latest generation

The use of computers to calculate the complex curvature and focal length of optical lenses and to control cutting and polishing has meant that telescopic sights can now be manufactured faster, more cheaply and to a degree of accuracy that was impossible 50 years ago. Variable magnification has long been available, but wide angle fixed 10x power scopes are now being fitted as standard to some service sniping rifles. Lens coatings, using technology borrowed from camera manufacturers, give more efficient light absorption in low light conditions and reduced glare in bright sunlight, giving the sniper better vision and faster target location. More importantly, the old problem of estimating ranges has been solved by the introduction of a whole family of laser rangefinders.

The Bushnell Yardage-Pro series, the size of a pair of compact binoculars, can measure ranges up to 1,200 metres with an accuracy of ±1 metre. Rangefinders small enough to be fitted onto a rifle are already in production, and miniaturisation will ensure that within a very short time such technology will become integral to telescopic sights. If estimating the range of a target is becoming easier, so is seeing it at night. The Starlight night vision sights used in the Vietnam War proved invaluable, but their performance was limited. New third generation night vision sights such as Honeywell's Short Range Thermal Sight have overcome these limitations by using thermal imaging. No matter how well an enemy soldier may be camouflaged on a moonless night, he will show up clearly as his body temperature effectively makes him appear to glow in the dark.

OPPOSITE **US Special Forces sniper team in Iraq, February 1991. The sniper holds a 7.62mm Remington M24 SWS rifle with 10x power Leupold Ultra M3A sight. The SWS has a fitted bipod, necessary due to its near-14lb (6.3kg) weight. A fully equipped M24 currently costs $3,980, but is not available commercially. (Courtesy Remington Arms Company)**

Neither does technology stop with electronics. Rifle mechanisms incorporate innovative component designs, and barrel life and accuracy have benefited enormously from new steel technology and computer designed rates of rifling twist designed for different sniping applications. Some US Remington M24 sniping rifles have fired over 5,000 rounds without any noticeable reduction in accuracy. A greater understanding of the effects of supersonic flight on bullets has also led to improvements in ballistic design and propellants. Specially designed ammunition with ballistic performance very close to that of ordinary supersonic ammunition is now available for suppressed ('silenced') sniping rifles. This means that rifle performance is no longer compromised, enabling silent shooting to be undertaken at far greater ranges than ever before. In practice all these technological advances mean that a modern sniping rifle is approximately four times more accurate than its equivalent at the start of World War I. It is now possible to produce a .223in (5.56mm) bolt action sniping rifle, traditionally regarded as too light for anything but moderate-range shooting, that is capable of firing accurately out to 1,000 metres. This was not considered technically feasible 25 years ago.

Since the Vietnam War there has been a steady movement away from using modified infantry rifles for fulfilling sniping roles. The United States adopted the purpose designed and built Remington M24 SWS in 1988; and in an unusual move, the British Royal Marines have just purchased 44 Accuracy International AWM rifles. These are equipped with Simrad nightsights and chambered for the potent .338in Lapua Magnum cartridge, the calibre giving the rifle a 1,500+ yard capability. This is the first time a service rifle has been adopted that uses a non-military calibre, and is perhaps a portent of the direction in which sniping rifle development is heading. There has also been a rapid growth in 'anti-matériel' sniping rifles of very large calibre, .50in or even 20mm. These are used for the long-range neutralisation of vital installations such as rocket launchers, command posts, radio communication centres or static enemy vehicles or aircraft. They are thus a classic 'force multiplier' for the type of relatively small spearhead unit whose rapid

The AWM rifle recently adopted in .338in Lapua Magnum calibre by the British Royal Marines. The .338 gives first hit probability out to 1,100+ metres without the weight and recoil penalty of the .50in Browning cartridge as used in the Barrett. This example has the optional Simrad KN200 nightsight fitted. (Courtesy Accuracy International)

A .50 calibre Barrett M90A1 rifle, one of the new breed of 'anti-matériel' weapons. This bolt action bullpup design is shorter and lighter than the semi-automatic M82A1. At 22lbs (9.98kg) it is still no lightweight, and its very efficient muzzle brake and high density shock-absorbing butt pad reduce its recoil to manageable proportions. (Courtesy the Trustees of the Royal Armouries, object no.XII.11067)

deployment to distant battlefields plays a major part in modern military operations. One sniper with such a rifle can effectively knock out light armoured vehicles from almost a mile away – as Sgt Kenneth Terry of the 3/1st US Marines proved in February 1991 during the Gulf War. Using a .50 calibre Barrett M82A1, he halted an Iraqi YW531 armoured personnel carrier with two armour-piercing/incendiary rounds at a range of 1,100 metres; the crews of two other APCs accompanying it very sensibly surrendered.

In recent years most of the major Western powers have begun to look hard at the demands placed on their snipers and at the weapons supplied to them. Modern wars are very different from the conflicts of half a century ago. Increasingly, as has been seen in Northern Ireland, terrorists may have access to sniping weapons with a performance that regular armies cannot match, leaving them powerless to respond. The rise of terrorism as a political force, and recent wars in a dozen places around the globe, have proved that weapons technology is available to anyone with the money to buy it, and Western governments ignore the fact at their peril. The amount of research and development time being devoted to this problem is perhaps a sign that sniping has finally been recognised as a necessary and vital battlefield function. One thing is certain: that on the battlefield of the future it will not be possible to hide from the sniper.

SELECT BIBLIOGRAPHY

Adrian Gilbert, *Sniper One-to-One*, Sidgwick & Jackson (1994)
Adrian Gilbert, *Stalk and Kill*, Sidgwick & Jackson (1997)
Major Hesketh-Pritchard, *Sniping in France*, Hutchinson (1919)
Ian V.Hogg, *The World's Sniping Rifles*, Greenhill Books (1998)
Ed Kugler, *Dead Centre*, Ivy Books (1999)
Michael Lee Lanning, *Inside the Crosshairs*, Ivy Books (1998)
H.W.McBride, *A Rifleman Went to War*, Lancer Militaria (1988)
Peter R.Senich, *The German Sniper*, Paladin Press (1982)
Peter R.Senich, *The Pictorial History of US Sniping*, Paladin Press (1980)
Peter R.Senich, *The Long Range War*, Paladin Press (1994)
Captain C.Shore, *With British Snipers to the Reich*, Paladin Press (1988)
Ian Skennerton, *The British Sniper*, Arms & Armour Press (1983)
Barry Wynn, *The Sniper*, Macdonald (1966)

THE PLATES

A1: Captain, Gloucestershire Regiment, British Expeditionary Force; Flanders, 1915

During a quiet period in the trenches an infantry company commander prepares to try his luck at sniping – his weapon suggests a peacetime interest in big game hunting. It is a privately purchased Jeffery-Farquharson in .450in calibre, powerful enough to penetrate the steel plates behind which the German snipers also worked. His only deviations from standard service dress are the inelegant but practical black rubber 'gumboots'. He still wears cuff rank insignia, a practice gradually abandoned – like the Sam Browne belt equipment, and even the officers' service jacket and breeches – once it was realised that they made officers an identifiable prey for enemy snipers. In 1915 the steel 'shrapnel helmet' was not yet available, and head wounds from sniping were common. His own steel loophole plate has no light-proof backing screen, and will show up as a bright spot as soon as he opens the covert to take aim, instantly advertising his position to any sharp-eyed German. Snipers quickly learned to build a blanket-covered framework around their posts to avoid this, and to angle their loopholes so as to prevent observation from directly in front.

A2: British infantry scout-sniper; Arras, 1917

By 1917 the British sniper had learned his trade very effectively, and had turned the tables on his German counterparts. Snipers now wore clothing specifically adapted to their needs; this man has made himself a 'ghillie suit' from hessian (burlap) material. Typically these had small pieces torn from sand bags and bunches of string or unravelled rope sewn to them to soften their outline and allow them to blend with the background. He has chosen to wear a knitted 'cap, comforter' but has camouflaged his head further with fine netting; his hands are covered with hessian mittens but leaving his trigger finger free. He aims a Mk III Short Magazine Lee-Enfield rifle fitted with an Aldis Mk III telescopic sight on an offset mount.

A3: Sergeant observer, King's Royal Rifle Corps, 41st Division; Western Front, 1917

Realism obviously conflicts with the need to illustrate clearly: here we choose to show a uniform fully badged and uncovered, though striped with shadows – in reality both members of a sniper team would conceal themselves much better than this, and would expect to remain in their positions throughout the daylight hours. In the ruins of a shelled cottage this sergeant keeps watch through a 20x power telescope, and takes notes; he would actually be better hidden in the dark recesses of the wreckage to prevent the lens catching the light. For this duty both men would probably leave off their steel helmets – which anyway gave no protection against high velocity rifle bullets – and also their puttees. He wears the 1917 soft cap, and on his sleeves he displays the battle badge of 18th Bn KRRC. Given the Rifles' strict tradition of wearing all buttons and badges in black, we have blackened the scouts' brass fleur-de-lys worn above the rank chevrons on his right arm.

B1: Sniper team, German Jäger-Bataillon Nr.8; Alsace, spring 1915

The mass mobilisation of 1914 naturally somewhat diluted the special quality of the peacetime Jäger battalions recruited from foresters and other countrymen, among whom there was a long tradition of marksmanship; nevertheless, in early 1915 some echo of the old expertise still set them apart. The 8th, a Rhineland unit, fought in Alsace under XV Korps, and distinguished itself in April in the fighting for a dominating 2,100-foot feature called the Hartsmannswillerkopf. In a quieter period, this marksman and his observer have virtual mastery of No Man's Land; at this date German snipers were shooting at long enough range not to have to fear retaliation in kind. He is using a commercially manufactured Mauser sporting rifle in 7.92mm service calibre, equipped with a 4x power scope. The observer has issue 6x30 binoculars, which were adequate for short to medium ranges (up to 500 metres) but lacked the range and clarity of British spotting telescopes. Both wear the 1907/10 uniform in the Jägers' distinctive *Graugrun* piped with dark green. The sniper has laid his shako in its canvas cover on the parapet (remarkably, the tall cockade was not ordered removed until that September), together with the binocular case; a cotton bandoleer hangs from the characteristically neat German brushwood trench revetting.

OPPOSITE **France, 1918: an American Expeditionary Force sniper (left) holds a M1903 Remington equipped with a Warner & Swasey sight. The apparent unease of this group is possibly caused by the soldier at the right, who seems to be about to juggle with a pair of hand grenades... (Courtesy US Army Military History Institute)**

RIGHT **'Somewhere in Italy', 1944: a US Army sniper takes a moment to clean his Springfield M1903A-4. The M1907 leather sling was a vital piece of the sniper's equipment; wrapped around the upper left arm and under the left wrist, it enabled a far steadier aim. The lack of iron sights on these rifles was a distinct disadvantage. (Courtesy US Army Military History Institute)**

Waffen-SS sniper taking aim with a long Great War-vintage Gewehr 98 rifle, fitted with a contemporary telescopic sight. As the rifle's safety catch is on we may safely assume that this was a posed photo for the benefit of the camera; few snipers would want a cameraman anywhere near them when working ... Compare with Plate E2 for uniform detail. (Courtesy Bundesarchiv)

B2: German infantry Scharfschütze, France 1918

This scene would really take place before dawn. Equipped with an issue Scharfschützen-Gewehr 98 rifle and 3x power Zeiss scope, this sniper is making use of one of the many ingenious camouflaged positions that were built along the front lines – a canvas 'dead horse' built on a metal framework with straw stuffing, preferably sited among real dead horses. After installing himself under cover of darkness, with a small supply of food and water and a dozen rounds of Sm.K armour-piercing ammunition, he will not leave the hide until nightfall. He has not adopted camouflage clothing, but wears the standard M1915 pattern blouse and M1916 helmet; his position is very unlikely to be spotted unless he gives himself away by his own carelessness. By firing from within the cavity he is unlikely to betray himself by muzzle flash or smoke; he will probably fire only four or five careful shots in a day, and will be careful not to compromise such an excellent position.

C1: Sniper, Japanese Special Naval Landing Forces; Pacific, 1943-45

The *Rikusentai* or naval infantry justified their elite reputation when serving as garrisons throughout Japan's fiercely defended Pacific empire, from Tarawa to the Philippines. This sniper displays their yellow anchor cap badge and the sleeve rank patch of *suihai-cho* (leading seaman). Although not highly trained snipers – they were taught to shoot only to moderate ranges – the Japanese were masters of camouflage and suicidally brave, often courting certain death to ensure that they hit their chosen target. This man is armed with the 6.5mm Type 97 rifle with a 2.5x power scope. This was unusual in having no elevation or windage adjustment, the crosshairs in the reticule being graduated for range and windage. This odd system, allied to the low magnification, would have made it a very difficult scope to use over about 400 metres. By definition, there is little photographic evidence of Japanese snipers' appearance when in place in their brilliantly concealed spider-hole or treetop hides; our figure is necessarily reconstructed largely from descriptions. As seems to have been usual, he works alone. He climbs with a strap of linked waist belts, and climbing irons tied to his

canvas and rubber *tabi* divided-toe shoes. His M1938 cap has a neck curtain of cotton strips; once in place he will put on his steel helmet, which is covered with cloth, a large-mesh string net, and local foliage; he will also conceal his face with a mosquito net. The M1933 naval infantry uniform was of a slightly greener tint of khaki than that of the army, though late in the war all shades were seen; and by this date the canvas gaiters formerly special to the naval troops had generally been replaced by puttees.

Fastened only at the neck and chest while he climbs, his camouflage cloak, made up of a separate cape and a body apron, is shown here as locally made from *attap*; it is based on the early-war issue sniper's cloak made of feathery green cotton fibres, which would probably not have been available in far-flung garrisons by this date. (All such garments were based on the centuries-old Japanese rain cape made of rice straw.) Apart from ammunition and a water bottle he would take only minimal equipment into the treetops; we show a safety rope with which he will tie himself to the tree, the case for his scope sight, and a small bag with his most precious and sacred personal effects – he does not expect to come down alive.

C2 & C3: US Army sniper team, Pacific, 1944-45

This sergeant sniper and his observer from an 8th Army unit are pinned down by enemy fire during the campaign to liberate the Philippines; the observer prepares to try an old but still effective trick to draw enemy fire, while the sniper adjusts the M82 scope on his semi-automatic M1C Garand. Although heavy, the M1C was liked by snipers for its ease of use. However, it could only be loaded with a full eight-round clip; the rifle could not then be reloaded until empty. The ejection of the clip with the last empty cartridge made a tell-tale 'ping', and this could prompt a Japanese rush – to guard against this the observer is armed with a .45cal M1A1 Thompson sub-machine gun with 20-round magazines.

The almost universal combat dress in the Pacific was the M1943 drab green herringbone twill fatigues (HBTs), but the sergeant has acquired the jacket from the M1942 two-piece camouflage uniform. This, and the preceding one-piece camouflage suit, was still worn to some extent by snipers and scouts. No marks of rank were worn in the field, to avoid the sharp eyes of Japanese snipers. The M1941 HBT fatigue cap and a pair of 'rough-out' boots complete the outfit. His equipment is limited to the M1938 dismounted cartridge belt with first aid pouch and canteen, and he carries extra ammunition in a cotton bandoleer.

His observer wears the full HBT uniform, with M1942 canvas and rubber jungle boots. His M1936 pistol belt supports both the standard aid pouch and the more comprehensive 'jungle' version; and a five-pouch carrier for Thompson magazines.

D: Soviet Red Army snipers, Russian Front, 1943-44

Red Army snipers were the scourge of the Wehrmacht on their Eastern Front, and – alone among the combatant nations – Russia encouraged women to train for this role in large numbers. They proved very effective; for instance, D1 is based on the accompanying portrait photograph of Senior Sergeant Roza Shanina. At least two and possibly three distinct types of camouflage suit were issued to scouts and snipers during the war years, apart from white over-garments for winter. This one-piece overall in a 'cloud' pattern was the first type, and was produced in both this scheme of brown on light khaki and in black on light olive drab. A fine net mask was often worn under the large hood, rendering the face virtually invisible. She carries here a 7.62mm Moisin-Nagant M91/30 rifle fitted with a 4x power PT scope sight.

Figure D2, a male sniper in 1944, wears the standard M1940 steel helmet, and a second pattern of camouflage suit called the *mochalniy*. Like that worn by D1, this was cut extremely loose and with a very large hood so that it could be worn over any other uniform and equipment. This two-piece suit in light olive drab relied not upon a printed pattern but upon permanently attached camouflage material to break up the outline. It was made with lengths of cotton tape sewn at regular intervals along the vertical seams of the smock and trousers, and bunches of false grass made of dyed raffia were knotted to these. Cloth loops across the chest and thighs were also provided so that additional local foliage could be attached. His weapon is the 7.62mm M1940 Tokarev semi-automatic rifle with a 3.5x power PU scope; this is clamped onto a U-shaped mounting bracket that locks on to the receiver from the rear.

E1: Sniper, German 2.Fallschirmjäger-Division; Dutch/German border, winter 1944

The Germans were the first country to produce camouflage-printed combat clothing as general issue to infantry, and during World War II they manufactured far more variants than any other combatant nation. The Luftwaffe paratroopers of the Fallschirmjäger divisions were equipped with camouflage helmet covers, jump-smocks and even ammunition bandoleers from 1941; this sniper's smock, in Luftwaffe 'splinter' pattern, is not special to his function. By the time 2.FJD – wiped out at Brest in September 1944 – had been re-formed in Holland, they were paratroopers in name only, and many airborne items were being replaced with Wehrmacht general issue. Though the smock was still common, this soldier typically wears field grey trousers, canvas anklets and ordinary ankle boots. Fighting as a

The Red Army successfully employed many women snipers. This is Senior Sergeant Roza Shanina, who was credited with 54 kills. She holds a M1891/30 Mosin-Nagant with the 3.5x PU scope, and wears the decoration of the Order of Glory. See Plate D1. (Courtesy Arkhiv Muzeya Panorami Stalingradskoy Bitvi)

conventional infantryman, he has opted for a standard M1943 helmet rather than the less protective rimless paratrooper's type; he has tied on a rough cover of sacking to kill reflections and break up the outline, and has added foliage from around his position.

He is using an issue 6x30 monocular to search for targets for his 7.92mm Mauser K98k. This is fitted with the unusual, quickly detachable 1.5x power Zielfernrohr 41 scope. Never regarded by snipers as a 'serious' telescopic sight, with its very long eye relief and tiny field of view, it was useful when nothing else was available; and curiously, more ZF41s were manufactured than any other type. The sight's protective case is carried on his belt.

E2: Sniper, German 6.SS-Gebirgs-Division 'Nord'; North Russia, 1943

The Waffen-SS were the first troops to receive camouflage-printed clothing as general issue; the first patterns of their smocks, helmet covers and face masks were ordered in June 1938. This division, mauled in Lapland in June 1941 and withdrawn for retraining and re-equipment, returned to the front in August 1942. Although nominally a mountain division, it saw most combat in the low-lying Baltic coast sector. This sniper, concealed in boggy ground, wears a newly issued 'second pattern' smock and helmet cover, both with foliage loops, in the so-called 'ringed oakleaf' pattern. The string face mask – originally pronounced useless in 1939 – was finally given a limited issue from April 1942, and was well suited to sniping. His Mauser K98k is fitted with a Mauser-manufactured 4x power scope on a double-claw mounting peculiar to Waffen-SS rifles.

F: British sniper team; NW Europe, autumn 1944

To the envy of many of their comrades, the snipers of British infantry battalions were not only excused most routine duties but were also permitted to wear any form of issue clothing they found suitable. This sniper F1, patiently watching from his hide well back from the holes in the roof of a damaged house, wears over his battledress the camouflage-printed version of the 'windproof' suit in light cotton material. This four-pocket, hooded, pullover smock and loose trousers saw widespread issue as over-garments to infantry in the last months of the war, but were already popular with snipers; some used them as the basis for home-made ghillie suits. He has spread his camouflage face veil, of green- and brown-printed netting, over his head and shoulders; this was in fact the intended purpose of an item which saw more general use as a scarf. He has a minimum of equipment – a waterbottle, and a 50-round cotton bandoleer; his capacious pockets can hold a compass, ammunition, spare parts tin, maps, sweets, etc. His rifle is the .303in Enfield No.4 Mk I (T), with a No.32 Mk II 3x power sight (the T denotes the rifle's conversion for telescopic sights).

The sniper's partner F2 has acquired a paratrooper's 1941 pattern Denison smock, which offers many of the same advantages as the windproofs. Few snipers wore steel helmets; this soldier wears his rolled woollen 'cap, comforter'. He too has minimal equipment – binoculars, and a few magazines stuck in his pockets. Although he is also a trained sniper he carries for convenience and firepower a Sten 9mm sub-machine gun, and may have a grenade or two in his pockets. His job is to watch for and identify targets, but also to ensure that the team do not become victims of localised counter-attacks in the hard street fighting characteristic of the British advance across Belgium and Holland.

G1: Sniper, Royal Australian Regiment, 1st Commonwealth Division; Korea, summer 1952

As in other wars, Australians showed themselves to be very adept at sniping, combining a hunting tradition of marksmanship with a self-reliant attitude. In a quiet period this Aussie has taken up position in a foxhole on the edge of a sandbagged company area on a hilltop overlooking North Korean lines. Clothing, as always, was left very much up to the individual; the 'Digger's' characteristic slouch hat was usually retained, but he has 'borrowed' an American M1951 armour vest – the first general issue 'flak jacket'. His weapon is a .303in Enfield No.3 Mk I* (T) of 1918 vintage, arguably the best Allied sniping rifle to emerge from the Great War. The No.4 (T) was also in use, but some snipers preferred the smoother Mauser action and less troublesome windage and elevation system of the older Aldis scope.

A fine informal portrait of sniper Private Francis Miller, 5th Bn, East Yorkshire Regiment, British 50th Infantry Division. He wears light fighting order comprising the ever-popular Denison smock apparently with camouflaged, windproof trousers. Frank Miller was known as 'Borrowed Time' as he was the only one of 12 battalion snipers to survive the 5th East Yorks' advance across France and the Low Countries into Germany in 1944-45. He won the Military Medal for his sniping exploits. See Plate F. (Courtesy Imperial War Museum, neg. B11098)

G2: British 22nd Special Air Service Regiment; Oman, early 1970s

This SAS soldier is serving with the British Army Training Team (BATT) in Dhofar province, with the forces of the reformist Sultan Qaboos, against Yemeni-backed guerrillas of the Popular Front for the Liberation of Oman and the Arabian Gulf (PFLOAG) – referred to as the *adoo*. Typically, he wears a cut-down floppy-brimmed bush hat; a windproof camouflage smock, much faded in use and modified with a front zip fastener (these World War II era garments had a certain 'folklore' cachet); light drab green trousers, and commercial boots which were more durable than the issue item. His 'belt order' is individually made up using mostly British 1958 pattern items with some US and West German additions; visible are two British 1944 waterbottles. Beards and uncut hair were typically worn for operations with the *firqat* – gangs of 'turned' guerrillas who were led back into the desert hills to track down their former comrades. To neutralise a well-hidden *adoo* sniper among the rocks he uses a Carl Gustav recoilless rifle, officially the '84mm Infantry Anti-Tank Gun', which could fire a 5.7lb (2.6kg) HE round out to 1,000 metres with devastating effect. Well-made and reliable, at 36lbs (16.3kg) it was very heavy, and it had a fearsome 30m backblast with discharge concussion that could loosen the firer's teeth.

H: US 5th Marines sniper team; I Corps Tactical Zone, South Vietnam, 1970

A Marine sniper uses the only firm support he can find for long-range shooting from the tree cover at the edge of a paddy field. (He is just preparing to aim, or recovering from a shot, since the free-floating barrel would never be rested for shooting – only its wooden furniture.) While the Marines prided themselves on their discipline in contrast to the US Army, scout-snipers enjoyed a good deal of latitude; H1 wears only the T-shirt, tropical fatigue trousers and nylon and leather jungle boots, with a bandage acting as a sweat-rag round his head and a towel round his neck. He carries minimal kit: a belt with two canteens and an aid pouch, with the rest of his necessities in a Claymore bag and a bandoleer. His weapon is the 7.62mm M40 (M700 Remington) with a Redfield 3x/9x ART II variable power scope which incorporated a self-ranging system, permitting very accurate judgement of distances. His observer and temporary barrel rest, H2, wears an unconventional mix of clothing: the newer leaf-pattern camouflage 'boonie hat' and 1968 trousers with the older green utility shirt, and a modified M1955 'flak jacket' – generally unpopular for its weight and heat. By means of their hooks and a cord he has attached to its lower edge eyelets his canteens, aid pouch, and the ammo pouches for his M14 rifle – out-dated, but still preferred over the M16 by sniper teams, since it had twice the range, and shared the same ammunition as the M40.

I1: Sniper, British Parachute Regiment; Falkland Islands, 1982

Because of the largely featureless and uninhabited terrain of the Falklands, and the advancing and attacking nature of British operations, snipers operated with the rest of their battalions, being called upon to deal with opposition as and when it was met. Like any other Para of 2nd or 3rd Battalion, this sniper has been 'tabbing' under a massive load of kit; some carried up to 150lbs (86 kg). He tops this with a rolled foam rubber sleeping mat, a useful item when lying on hard ground observing for any length of time. He wears the 'Arctic windproof' suit in DPM camouflage over quilted liners. Regimental pride dictates the wearing of the beret under all possible circumstances, but his helmet is slung on his pack;

Two British snipers clad in white snowsuits crawl cautiously to the edge of a wood somewhere on the Dutch/German border, early 1945. The lead man has a Mk V Sten gun with bayonet attached, while the sniper holds his No.4 (T) in readiness. The American M1907 leather sling can clearly be seen fitted to the sniper's Enfield. (Courtesy Imperial War Museum, neg. B13664)

he has camouflaged it with hessian, net and 'scrim'. He has done the same to the barrel of his weapon – the L42 rifle, which is fitted with the improved Mk III version of the World War II No.32 scope. These scopes were supposedly specially sealed to prevent moisture ingress, but it was not always successful. Against the wet of the Falklands winter he keeps the leather protective caps on until the last moment, and is covering his rifle muzzle with tape.

I2: Sniper, Argentine Regimiento (Especial) de Infanteria 25; Islas Malvinas, 1982

Since he is risking his life to hold the islands, it seems only courteous to use the name by which he has always known them: men of Co.C/RI25 fought with courage, perseverance and effectiveness at San Carlos and Goose Green. This is a career NCO, one of the cadre of a regiment that received a good deal of special forces training under the energetic command of LtCol Mohamed Ali Seineldin. He wears an Israeli-made parka with a national patch on the left sleeve – an unofficial but common insignia in this unit. The green fatigues and Tempex nylon belt equipment are standard issue; and the excellent Argentine waterproof boots were much envied by British servicemen. The US M1 helmet (worn here

over the Argentine winter cap) was universal, but the US Army leaf pattern camouflage cover was a peculiarity of RI25 – as was the regiment's non-regulation green velveteen beret with brass '25' over the infantry's crossed rifles badge, here thrust into his cargo pocket. Rifles varied widely: some snipers were issued the Argentine-made Mauser K98k and scopes of World War II vintage. However, this soldier has one of the most modern systems of its date – a National Match M14 rifle equipped with a bulky but effective American AN/PVS-2 night sight. With this combination many Argentine snipers gave the British forces a great deal of trouble during night assaults.

J1: Sniper, Soviet 103rd Guards Air Assault Division; Afghanistan, 1985

This *desantnik* sniper, unexpectedly pinned down during a joint operation with Afghan government forces, wears the Red Army's cold weather *ushanka* cap in grey cloth and synthetic fleece, and the padded winter version of the standard khaki field uniform with a grey 'fish fur' collar. As a paratrooper he has received body armour; this was eventually adopted by most troops serving in Afghanistan. Paratroopers usually operated from assault helicopters and were lightly equipped. He carries the semi-automatic

OPPOSITE **A British SAS soldier in Dhofar province, Oman, c1974; see Plate G2. He carries an L42 rifle and has a US M79 grenade launcher on his pack. Although they had specialist snipers, all SAS men were trained in the use of the L42.**

US Army snipers posed for the camera in Vietnam, October 1969 – the fatigues are impossibly clean for an operational photo. These snipers both carry National Match M14 rifles; at right, the telescopic sight is an M84 of World War II vintage. The standing soldier's M14 has the side rail fitting for the Starlight infra-red night vision sight. (Courtesy US National Archives)

Dragunov SVD rifle, with its PSO scope, which proved an excellent combination for shooting out to 800 or 900 metres. Although the Soviets had more 20th-century sniping experience than any other European army, and their snipers were well equipped, they had serious problems combating the Afghan *mujahideen* sharpshooters. Intimate knowledge of the terrain, acute eyesight, natural skill and an age-old tribal culture of guerrilla marksmanship made them fearsome adversaries even when they carried such relative antiques as the .303in SMLE. The Russians later formed special counter-sniper squads equipped with RPG rocket-launchers; as the British had found out in Arabia some years earlier, such weapons can be highly effective in this role.

J2: Sniper, French 2e Régiment Étranger d'Infanterie; IFOR, Bosnia, winter 1995

The French did not field many snipers during the two World Wars, but their post-war colonial experiences in Indochina and Algeria caused a rapid reassessment of the requirement. Unlike other NATO countries they decided to have a trained sniper working as a member of each infantry section, a doctrine that seems to work well. During the recent siege of Sarajevo local snipers murdered many civilians as they went about their desperate daily search for food and water. Since their deployment in 1992 the French UN contingents have tried to discourage these killers, although the weak UNPROFOR mandate forbade UN troops to fire unless fired upon themselves. In 1995 LtCol Lecerf's 2nd Foreign Infantry Regiment played an active part in breaking the siege; and the hand-over of responsibility to the NATO-led IFOR, which saw the end of blue helmets and white vehicles, ushered in much more robust rules of engagement. This légionnaire, a section sniper whose coloured shoulder scarf identifies the 2e REI's 1st Company, reports in from an urban position. He wears a Spectra helmet and body armour covered in the then-new French camouflage pattern over his green fatigues. He uses the MAS36-based 7.62mm FR-F2 bolt action sniping rifle equipped with M53bis scope, which he rests on its bipod on a blanket-covered table; his loophole is disguised with a slit blanket; and above it is a composite panoramic photo of the cityscape opposite, on which successive watches will note their accumulated intelligence about the enemy's favoured haunts and routes.

K1: Sniper, US Army Special Forces; Gulf War, 1990–91

The US forces had for some time been testing the new generation of heavy sniping rifles designed around the .50cal round for the Browning M2 machine gun. In addition to anti-personnel use, in which role they are naturally devastating, their long range and a variety of armour-piercing and incendiary rounds give them great potential for destroying enemy transport, parked aircraft, telecommunications gear, and even light armoured vehicles. Although desert warfare does not usually give snipers much chance to use their skills, some remarkable results were achieved in the Gulf. This NCO sniper of the 'Green Berets' carries the single-shot Research Armament Industries M500, with an effective range of 1,800 metres; it is unusual in that the bolt must be removed for reloading after each shot. He wears a bandana, Desert Battle Dress Uniform without insignia, a home-made ghillie suit of burlap strips on tan netting, and the sand-coloured version of the new IIFS gear which was issued to Special Forces.

K2 & K3: US Marine sniper team; Gulf War, 1991

The Marines wore DBDUs but with PASGT body armour covers and ALICE personal gear still in temperate climate camouflage – desert versions were not yet available to them. K2, the observer of the two-man team, uses the battle-proven 20x power M49 spotting telescope, which had been in service since Vietnam; its M15 tripod is occasionally seen in photos used as a rifle rest for Marine snipers' M40 Remingtons.

The sergeant sniper, K3, wears a 'Fritz' helmet and ALICE gear, but has discarded the body armour for comfort when shooting. Jungle boots were standard USMC issue, but proved less than ideal in the desert – they let in too much sand and heat. His weapon is the M82A1 Barrett 'Light Fifty' with a ten-round magazine, fitted with an Unertl 10x power scope, of which 100 were rushed to scout-sniper platoons in Saudi Arabia before they had been fully tested by the USMC. Despite some teething troubles, the combination proved

A nod to an earlier age of sniping, which still proved as potent in the 1980s against the Soviet Army as it had in the 1920s and 30s against the British. These Afghan tribesmen carry the Short Magazine Lee Enfield; taught to shoot from childhood, they are masters of natural camouflage and totally at home in their arid mountain environment. They have never been defeated by a modern invading army. (Courtesy Imperial War Museum, neg.Q70635)

extremely effective. The big .50cal cartridge, with its remarkably flat trajectory and low recoil (25.9ft/lbs), made engaging targets at 1,400-1,500 metres entirely possible, but shooting at these ranges in the desert brings its own problems. Apart from heat distortion and strong winds, simply identifying the target at nearly a mile demands a scope of at least 10x power magnification.

L: Snipers' lairs; France, summer 1944

This aerial view of an imaginary French village and its surroundings shows the type of scenario in which snipers operated extensively during the heavy fighting in North-West Europe in 1944-45. This landscape offers many good sniping positions. Wherever possible snipers chose high ground, giving themselves better fields of observation and fire. There were certain places that few snipers would risk using, however. Tall man-made structures such as church spires (1) and water towers (2) were attractive to the unwary sniper or artillery OP, but were therefore obvious aiming points for enemy artillery, and the first places that counter-snipers would look. The anonymous loft of a shell-damaged cottage (3) made a much safer place for a hide.

Taking up position in a lone building, such as an isolated château or farmhouse (4), was likely to lead to discovery and retaliation in the form of mortar and machine gun fire; establishing a camouflaged ground position some distance from it (5) would be far less likely to lead to detection. Wrecked vehicles could provide good cover (6), providing

A sight rarely seen by anyone who has lived to tell the tale: two British snipers in ghillie suits spot for targets. The soldier on the right has a fine mesh over the lens of his telescopic sight to prevent reflections. (Courtesy HQ Land Command)

that the sniper moved position frequently. Woodland and fields under crops (7) were better; their large size, close growth, and lack of specific features to draw the eye made locating snipers very difficult. There are many accounts of German snipers tying themselves into treetops in the Japanese style, and with the same ultimate results. The dense belts of hedgerow or *bocage* (8) so typical of north-west France were ideal for both sniper and tank-killer teams, who could fire and move on to a new position in moments. So costly did it prove to flush out German ambushers while channelled along the deep lanes that Allied tanks were fitted with improvised steel blades to smash paths through the banked hedgerows.

Crossroads (9) were also to be avoided. Clearly marked on maps, they were inevitably heavily shelled in the hope of catching convoys on the move. A position high up in a house a few hundred yards away overlooking a crossroads was ideal, however (10). Traffic police and officers' vehicles would provide excellent targets; and careless infantry units also tended to halt at crossroads to rest or await movement orders. Bridges (11) also offered good hunting, where a few well-placed shots could often cause havoc and long delays.

INDEX